A TEACHER'S GUIDE TO

Exciting Writing, Successful Speaking

Activities to Make Language Come Alive in the Classroom

Martin Kimeldorf

Edited by Pamela Espeland

Free Spirit
PUBLISHING

Cover and book design by MacLean & Tuminelly
Index prepared by Eileen Quam and Theresa Wolner

10 9 8 7 6 5 4 3 2 1

Printed in the United States of America

FREE SPIRIT PUBLISHING INC.
400 First Avenue North, Suite 616
Minneapolis, MN 55401
(612) 338-2068

Dedication

xciting Writing, Successful Speaking is dedicated to three important groups of people. First, my Uncle Alex, my wife, Judy, and other family members who supported my writing efforts. Second, my books have been enriched by the students and teachers who participated in the development of early drafts. Their feedback and encouragement were invaluable. Finally, I dedicate this work to publishers like Free Spirit, who honor the creativity and diversity of their readers and authors. And let me conclude with a special note of thanks to Pamela Espeland, who took my diamond-in-the-rough manuscript and polished it until it sparkled.

Contents

Introduction

*xciting Writing, Successful Speaking* was written in response to the traditional (and pedestrian) composition book I found myself teaching from in a high-school class. This is my alternative. The following principles guided me in its creation.

- Students respond best when assignments have interesting or provocative topics.

- Students are more serious about writing when they can work on projects or assignments related to real-world applications, or when they anticipate their work being seen, heard, or read by others.

- Students enjoy writing when it is presented in game-like or cooperative learning situations, or when they have some degree of choice in how they go about the learning task.

I wrote *Exciting Writing, Successful Speaking* to make writing come alive—to turn the skeleton of grammar and composition exercises into flesh-and-blood writing and communication experiences.

I originally consulted with two teachers who together possessed over 25 years of successful teaching experience in both regular and special education. I combined their suggestions with my own project-oriented handouts. Then I selected the items that my students found to be the most enjoyable (even exciting!). When all of these materials were adapted, revised, and organized, I resubmitted the work to my original consultants as well to as others in the field.

Everyone seemed to have a different angle on how to use the materials. Judy Kimeldorf used them in a middle-school program. Another teacher field-tested the materials in a special education resource room; a third used them in an alternative high school program; a fourth selected parts to enrich her high school program. Someone else suggested that there would be an audience for this work in adult basic education and English as a Second Language (ESL) programs.

You might then ask, "Are these materials for high school or middle school; special, regular, or alternative education; adult basic education or ESL?" The answer would be "Yes—to all." The activities and exercises have proven adaptable in ways I never conceived.

When I combined the materials in *Exciting Writing, Successful Speaking* with various composition assignments, I found that I had an excellent and flexible tool for language enrichment. For instance, I would begin with a journal-writing assignment which would last from one to two weeks, three to five days a week. Then I would stop and switch to short spelling and grammar exercises for 15 minutes per day, leaving the majority of the period for work on other units of instructions.

We also tackled full-time, one-to-two-week projects. Once each semester, we would shut down for seven to ten days and produce a class newsletter or poetry publication. Then we would return to our written language exercises. After completing several writing assignments, we would again stop and dip into the projects, exploring public speaking, drama activities, or survey-taking. The course always had plenty of variety with minimal effort on my part. At times, I used some of the literature-oriented worksheets that teach insights into the analysis of character, setting, and plot. I also consulted some of the recommended books listed in Suggested Readings and References at the end of this teacher's guide.

How This Program Is Organized

The lessons in *Exciting Writing, Successful Speaking* are grouped into three parts: (1) Exciting Writing; (2) Exciting Writing, Speaking and Reading; and (3) Exciting Reporting.

This Teacher's Guide contains tips and suggestions that will help you to prepare for each lesson. Many came from teachers who were involved in the field-testing of *Exciting Writing, Successful Speaking*. They include strategies for introducing the lessons, follow-up ideas, and ways to extend or enrich specific lessons. More tips are given for the beginning lessons in Part 1, because you might have more questions at this stage. Later, as you progress and adapt the material to your students' needs and your teaching style, you'll develop your own tips. Feel free to inquire about additional tips collected after the publication of *Exciting Writing, Successful Speaking*, and please send any new and exciting ideas to me.

At the end of this guide, you'll find several reproducible pages for student handouts. They include quizzes and other evaluation tools, forms for prewriting activities and organizational tasks, and various activity-type pages you may want to use more than once during the year. They are here to make your life easier. The Teacher's Guide sections that deal with the lessons include more details about the reproducible pages.

The student book provides everything your students need to learn and practice the skills and concepts presented in each lesson.

How to Use the Student Book and Teacher's Guide

The student book is a "workbook" in the traditional sense: it is meant to be written in, and each student will need his or her own copy.

You may use the student book in whatever way works best for you and your students. For example, you might hand out copies at the beginning of the school year as an enrichment tool to use in the classroom all year long. (If students dip into the materials on their own time, so much the better.) Or you might give them out at the start of each lesson and collect them at the end, directing your students' attention to the specific pages they will need for that lesson. Students can work in pairs or teams to complete the lessons. The student book is written in student-friendly language and is ideally suited both for independent and cooperative learning. (You will also discover that the materials are *teacher*-friendly. Even if you have never taught creative writing, speech, or report writing before now, *Exciting Writing, Successful Speaking* makes it easy to do.)

As a third option, you might treat the student lessons as "scripts" and present them orally to your students, pausing to let them work through the various activities and fill-in sections. The student text then becomes a set of "lecture notes" your students may refer to for review and reinforcement. Reading the lessons aloud is an especially powerful teaching technique to use with *Exciting Writing, Successful Speaking* because it makes the concepts, examples, and activities accessible to *all* students, even those with special learning needs.

In any case, be sure that students have their books to take home at the end of the school year. Include any related materials you haven't yet returned to them—completed handouts, quizzes, scripts, journals, and the like. Your students will then have a complete record of their *Exciting Writing* experience and progress, along with many useful materials, tips, ideas, and instructions for future reference.

Who knows—some students may decide to try some *Exciting Writing* during the summer. You might even encourage your students to do so. Judy Kimeldorf hands out self-addressed postcards at the end of the school year and invites her students to "send me a card if you do an assignment."

Other students with the writing bug may keep their student books and journals for years.

The Teacher's Guide is your permanent guide to the program. Refer to it whenever you teach *Exciting Writing, Successful Speaking.* As you teach, you may want to underline or highlight specific sections, write notes to yourself about the lessons, jot down new ideas, insert examples from your students, and otherwise customize this book so it becomes *your* Guide.

I encourage you to consider these materials as inherently flexible. Don't feel that you must present the lessons in order (although some do build on others, and these are clearly identified). Instead, skip around, pick and choose, modify and adapt.

Program Overview

Exciting Writing, Successful Speaking begins by addressing the problem that most of my students first face: how to get started on a page. List-making activities function as a simple and effective prewriting tool. Almost everyone has used lists at one time or another, and almost everyone agrees that they are easy to create (as compared to sentences or outlines). After list-making, a general four-step writing process is presented that emphasizes the brainstorming and organization skills associated with prewriting, drafting, and revising. These two beginning techniques are applicable to the various projects and assignments that follow.

The projects extend the writing experience through group or cooperative work and individual efforts. Often, they involve several learning objectives or competencies. For example, to write a good speech, one must use the critical skills of brainstorming, organizing, and visualizing. In the last step of speech-writing, the student tries to find a prop or story which will help to illustrate the speech topic. Writing out the speech addresses writing skills, while delivery involves the various public speaking competencies.

Students who complete a project experience the satisfaction of having produced something meaningful, and/or the thrill of sharing their work. Self-esteem grows. The projects add a final, vital link: a reason for writing besides just getting a grade.

I have found that students often enjoy repeating many of the projects on a regular basis. Poetry, journal writing, and script writing can be done over and over. For example, journal writing can be introduced early and kept as a daily, weekly, or frequent writing stimulus. Later, you can initiate a newsletter project and repeat it about once a quarter. (It takes me and my students about two weeks to go from choosing topics to writing and revising, keyboard entry, selection of graphics, layout with desktop publishing software, printing, and distribution.)

On the other hand, some projects, such as poetry or public speaking, might best be done a little at a time over a period of several weeks. Since reading is a nice break from writing, it might be useful to add in book reports, or to use the literature and story assignments for brief reading tasks involving magazines or short stories. Once the midyear doldrums set in, you'll find that drama or advertising assignments are fun to introduce (or bring back). In other words, you don't need to present the projects in any particular order, and you may return to them as many times as interest and outcome warrant.

You'll soon discover that these assignments and projects are accessible to almost all learners at various age and ability levels. Step-by-step directions, liberally illustrated with examples, help the student at each stage from conceptualization to finished product.

Grading and Reinforcement

Correcting and grading used to be hard for me because I always wanted to rewrite and edit out all the errors. Then one day a student said, "You're not going to mark that all up again! It took me over two hours to revise it last night." After that, I limited corrections to the first draft and focused on recognizing the efforts my students made in their final draft.

Many of my students often make new errors while correcting previous ones. As such, there is a limit to how much revising can be done before interest in writing is killed off. My best advice (which I must constantly give myself) is "Don't over-correct." Limit yourself to grading the big parts of each project, and limit the detailed corrections to the first draft. Only embarrassing things should be edited on the final draft. The emphasis should shift to reinforcement when the final draft is turned in.

As an alternative, you can set specific criteria for each writing assignment to match the major writing skill, rather than detecting and correcting every error. For example, after studying punctuation rules for using quotations, a writing assignment criteria for completion could be "The work must include three quotations." Then focus detection and correction on the three quotations and try to ignore other errors. (It's hard to do at first.) To reinforce writing efforts, I read students' final work out loud, have students send copies to other teachers or counselors, or post their work in class.

Mike Carlson, a teacher at Capital High School in Olympia, Washington, helped with some of the initial field-testing and review of *Exciting Writing, Successful Speaking*. His comments about grading are worth repeating here:

> Grading should foster success. If you correct every error in the rewritten draft, you'll find that it often contains as many errors as the first draft. Instead, use what I call a "holistic" approach to grading—

look at the paper as a whole. Pinpoint the main skill to be mastered in the lesson. When marking the first draft, show how the main skill can be achieved by revising. Be careful not to add too many markings or corrections as you look for secondary problems (like spelling or basic readability). I always allow students to revise their work until the criteria for the assignment is met. Finally, consider the student's overall effort in light of the assignment. Then write an encouraging note related to the student's effort—even when the final product falls short.

Let Me Know How It Works for You

I'm especially interested in any hints or suggestions you have for improving this program. (I also must rewrite.) Let me know if you would like to see your contributions (credited to you) included in the next revision of *Exciting Writing, Successful Speaking*. Send your ideas, samples, or questions to me at:

Free Spirit Publishing Inc.
400 First Avenue North, Suite 616
Minneapolis, MN 55401

I look forward to hearing from you.

Martin Kimeldorf
Tumwater, WA
Spring 1994

PART 1

Exciting Writing

Introduction

I f you plan to use a lot of the materials from *Exciting Writing, Successful Speaking,* you may wish to review all of the lesson introductions in the student book before you begin. This will give you a good overview of the program. If you are just trying one or two enrichment ideas at this time, then the introduction to that specific lesson may be sufficient. For your own purposes, you may still wish to read the student introductions.

Prior to starting *Exciting Writing, Successful Speaking,* you may want to lead your students in a brainstorming contest to see who can list the most ways of using writing in areas outside of school. Some examples might include:

- for personal growth or recreation: journals, graffiti, letters to friends

- on the job: reports, memos, advertising, letters

- in the arts: scripts, poems

- in public service or business: business letters, giving speeches.

List Writing

- List writing is a quick and easy brainstorming technique that can be used to help generate ideas during the prewriting stage.

- Students begin by identifying a leisure interest. Then they try to generate as many ideas as they can about their leisure interest within a specified time period. This is called Power Writing because setting a time limit is a powerful way to make a game out of generating ideas. Finally, students use their ideas to write a letter.

During the list writing activity, students can write down anything about their topic. They don't need to limit themselves to one aspect. They can take any slant on the subject they choose.

Power Writing is a powerful tool for generating lists. The best way to initiate writing begins with activity, energy, and focused "mind doodling" while ignoring the outcome or product. Worrying about the outcome can create writer's block. The sheer momentum of writing quickly can propel even the most reluctant writer. This simple and effective method can be used with many different assignments. I often ask my students to Power Write a list for one minute prior to starting a journal page.

Introduce Power Writing by doing an example on the board. Describe it as a word-association game. Start with a topic, such as a leisure activity. Then call on students to say the first word that comes to their mind. If they can't think of any words, they can call out "Blank" or their initials. Write down whatever they say (including "Blank" or their initials).

Afterward, have them Power Write on their own. Give them 2 minutes. Time them, have them time themselves, or assign a student to act as the timekeeper.

I have found that students enjoy counting their words after Power Writing. There are three ways to do this:

1. Count all lines or words, including the word "blank."

2. Count all words, excluding the word "blank."

3. Count all words, excluding the word "blank." Divide the total word count by 4 because it takes at least 4 ideas to create one paragraph. Then determine if Power Writing has produced enough ideas for the number of paragraphs needed.

Before beginning the letter writing activity, go over the general format of a personal letter—where to put the date, greeting, and closing. Then discuss how a letter of thanks usually not only thanks the person for a gift but also gives examples of how the gift will be used and/or reasons why the receiver likes the gift. You may want to compose a sample thank-you letter and write it on the board.

4-Step Writing

- 4-Step Writing takes students from prewriting to drafting and through revising and editing.

- Students learn 4-Step Writing by writing a movie critique. This is followed by a quiz on the process.

At first, 4-Step Writing may appear complicated, but rest assured that it has been carefully adapted from standard writing techniques and refined so it may be used by students of all ability levels. You may shorten the process or steps any way you wish. One simplification involves reducing the number of drafts or amount of input on step 3. For example, with students in special education, you may wish to omit the step of getting feedback from a peer (although most of my students enjoy this). Or you may want to have students make all of their changes on the first draft so they only have to create one more (final) draft.

This 4-Step system works because students get reinforcement, or "points," at short intervals. Feel free to adapt the point system anyway you choose. You may also want to modify the COPS checklist (see student book pages 15–16) to the level of grammar and punctuation expected for your students. My COPS list is purposefully limited to skills a student needs for self-editing. As a result, it may leave out grammar skills you want to emphasize, such as subject-verb agreement, the use of apostrophes, etc. The COPS system has proved very adequate for many students with special needs.

Specific lessons stand out when you apply special rewards. After students complete the movie review, consider a prize linked to the subject. For example, bring in a movie to show to the class. Or read aloud movie reviews printed in magazines and newspapers. Try to find reviews of movies students have seen. Ask whether they agree or disagree with the reviewers.

● ●

ABOUT THE HANDOUTS FOR THIS LESSON

● The 4-Step Writing Planning and Scoring Sheets
(pages 62–63) give your students a way to evaluate
their own writing efforts after completing the 4-Step
Writing exercise. You may want to collect the scoring
sheets along with the essays, write your scores along-
side theirs, and discuss any differences in follow-up
conferences.

● The 4-Step Writing Quiz (page 64) is designed for
success. The quiz is *not* graded.

● ●

Journal Writing

- Students learn how and why to keep journals, using almost any means of expression they choose (words alone, words and pictures, etc.). They learn how to begin and end a journal entry. A list of 101 Journal Writing Topics is found on pages 24–28 of the student book.

- Students learn six helpful journal writing rules. An optional Journal Word Count Chart gives them a way to track their progress and provides graphic evidence of the benefits of regular journal writing.

- Ideas for grading and correcting student journals which reinforce journal writing are provided, along with methods for enhancing the journal writing experience.

I get a lot of mileage out of having my students do journal writing. I learn a great deal about them through their journals, which helps me to establish a personal rapport with them. Meanwhile, my students are learning about an enjoyable form of recreational writing. Journals illustrate in concrete and immediate terms other benefits of writing which touch upon recreational and therapeutic outcomes.

There are many ways to introduce journal writing. For me, the best way is to model it by showing the class my own journals. (If you have no journals of your own, consider starting one.) I try to show that journals can be serious, whimsical, graphic, and crazy-fun. I show pages from my own journals with drawings, scrawled letters, doodles, etc. I joke about my drawings in order to encourage my students to draw or doodle. You might also try collecting sample journal writings from other students. In addition to sharing your own efforts, you will find that modeling journal writing behavior is a very powerful stimulus. Write in your own journal while your students are writing in theirs.

A good time allotment for daily journal writing is about 8-10 minutes. Add about 5 minutes to introduce the topic, brainstorm ideas, and count and chart the words (counting and charting are optional), and the total could be 15 minutes—a reasonable period to spend on such a rewarding and meaningful writing activity.

• •

ABOUT THE HANDOUT FOR THIS LESSON

The Journal Cover and Word Count Chart (page 65) may be used "as is" for student journals. Or students may want to design their own journal covers. You don't need to distribute the handout if you don't plan to use the word count chart in this lesson.

• •

Journal Topics

In the beginning, it's helpful for the teacher to suggest topics for the entire class. After writing the topic on the blackboard, we discuss possible ideas or points of view. I summarize the discussion-brainstorm by compiling a list of words. Students will often use these words to initiate writing and to assist in spelling.

I usually start our first journaling exercises with descriptive and concrete topics:

● *Describe your "dream machine"—the car you would own if money was no object.*

● *Describe what it's like when you wake up in the morning.*

● *Describe your best friend.*

Next, I move the topics toward age-appropriate concerns and controversies, or solicit advice:

● *Give advice on how to raise and train a pet.*

● *What's the best way to make friends?*

● *Where are the best places to eat out in this town? What kinds of food do they serve?*

Later, I introduce "emotional" topics about cafeteria food, school rules, laws, etc.:

● *Do you think school should start later and get out later or stay the same? Why?*

● *Should the driving age be lowered, raised, or kept the same?*

● *What school rule would you change, if you could?*

Once my students have developed a journal writing habit or routine, I reserve Mondays or Fridays for "personal feelings":

- *What are you feeling like today? What's on your mind?*
- *How has your day gone so far?*
- *What kind of mood are you in today? Why?*

A list of journal topics I have used successfully is found on pages 24–28 in the student book.*

Correcting, Grading, and Reinforcing Journal Writing Efforts

When looking at journals, keep corrections to a minimum—or even better, make none at all. I don't grade my students' journals. I simply grade their journal word count charts, when we use them. This grade usually combines a student self-evaluation with the average number of words charted.

More important than a grade or correction, I return their journals with two or more personal remarks. This makes it seem as though the writer and I are carrying on a conversation. My comments show that I have read the work and found it interesting. I'll write things like, "That's interesting," "Are you still angry?," "That was good advice you gave yourself," and "That meal sounds great—when do I get invited?" In fact, when I fail to write comments, many students get upset.

Finally, to help reinforce student efforts, I read passages out loud from student journals (after first asking their permission in private, and without revealing the writers' names). I try to highlight parts I like or feel illustrate good uses of a journal.

I ask everyone to draw a picture for their first three journal entries. That way, I can always comment on the drawing if the writing is not ready yet for exhibition.

Occasionally I get concerned about sloppy journal writing. When that happens, I circle errors and turn back the journals. Students must then rewrite and/or correct each line marked. Typical corrections include correcting spelling, fixing sentences that make no sense, and correcting basic grammar. I don't ask them to correct more than eight errors at a time.

---

* Three more excellent sources of journal topics are *The Kid's Book of Questions* by Gregory Stock (New York: Workman, 1988), which has never failed to stimulate interesting discussion in my classroom; *The Book of Questions* by the same author (Workman, 1987), a version for adults (and older students); and *Writing Down the Days: 365 Creative Journaling Ideas for Young People* by Lorraine M. Dahlstrom (Minneapolis: Free Spirit Publishing, 1990), with a year's worth of journaling ideas tied to the calendar. Also, I have written a book for adults called *w(Rites) of Passage: A Journal Writing Apprenticeship* that describes various journal writing techniques and applications for personal development. For more details, write to me c/o Free Spirit Publishing.

Using the Journal Word Count Chart

You will probably have many different goals for journal writing. One set of goals may emphasize writing practice and increasing output. Having your students write for a specified period of time each day (or every other day) and chart their total number of words is an effective way to achieve these goals.

Success is measured in two ways. First, I ask students to look at their word count charts. If their output has increased, this will be obvious from the charts. Almost all of my students tend to increase their word counts during the journal writing experience. We also discuss the fact that word counts will go up and down over time.

The second measure of success involves self-evaluation. I might ask, "Do you feel that journal writing has become easier or more interesting for you?" On this score, we get mixed reviews the first time self-evaluation is done.

I might also ask students to write a journal entry answering the question, "What grade should you get for journal writing and why?" Eventually you develop a feel for the amount of writing your students can comfortably complete in the allotted time. This helps to establish grading criteria based on word counts.

When I use the Journal Word Count Chart, I wait until students' charts are one-third to one-half full before evaluating them. Then I ask the students to interpret their own charts and journal writing efforts; this makes a good journal assignment. Afterward, I collect the charts for evaluation.

In special education classes for students with moderate to severe learning disabilities, you might allow 8-10 minutes for journal writing and use the following *suggested* grading criteria: 45-word averages earn a C; 46-65, a B; and above 65, an A.

An Alternate Approach

Your goal for journal writing may be to help your students find their own "voice." In this case, the amount of writing is not as important as the quality, and the Journal Word Count Chart is not needed.

I ask my students to pick a topic at the beginning of the week and write at least a half page (not more than a full page) by Friday, when they are expected to turn it in. They may choose their own time to write. I also encourage students to illustrate their work. For special needs students,

I allow a half page of writing and a half page of drawing or decoration. I often get spectacular results.

Whichever method you choose—charting words versus letting students work on their own—depends on what you want your students to achieve, and also on your personal teaching style or preference.

Enhancing the Journal Writing Experience

I often play music while students write. I begin with my music and later allow students to bring in their own audio cassettes. Music with offensive language or subject matter is not permitted. Music makes the journal part of the course seem special.

Don't do journals every day of the year. Take a break! My special ed students usually go for short periods of a time where they write for four to five days a week for two to three weeks. Then we take a two-week break and do spelling, short grammar reviews, or other short-term activities during the journal writing time slot.

When we leave our journals for a period of time, I try to personalize the experience by characterizing the journal as a friend. On the last day before "taking a vacation" from journal writing, students begin a journal entry with the words, "Dear Journal: I'll be leaving you for a while. I just wanted to say...." They write a short good-bye to their friend. (You'll be very surprised at what some will write.) Perhaps, when you return to journal writing, you can start them off with the line, "Hello, friend, it's good to see you again. I've got lots of things to tell you about...."

I also like to emphasize visual or graphic elements. I often bring in—or invite my students to bring in—pictures that they can paste into their journals and write about. My students who use the Journal Word Count Chart can add 10 points for any drawings or doodles added to a journal page. At times, I display their artwork in the classroom.

By the end of the year, you'll find that most students consider journal writing a special part of your course. In my second year, several students showed up with wire-bound notebooks so they could keep their journals intact. It was their own idea!

Advertising

- Students learn how to use language in a practical yet imaginative way in the form of persuasive advertising writing.

- Students begin by examining brief classified ads. They develop an awareness of the power of language to get the audience's attention. They learn to describe a product or service with convincing detail, and to give directions for acquiring the product or service.

- Students apply what they have learned so far by writing personal advertisements—a skill that links up nicely with résumé writing. They create a display or newspaper advertisement that combines words and pictures.

- Finally, students write scripts for radio and television advertisements.

Many of the activities in this lesson may be done in groups. After all, that's the way advertising agencies work!

You may want to return to these activities on several occasions during the year. Holidays are excellent times to practice advertising writing. My students enjoy writing ads for their moms on Mother's Day, and personal ads on Valentine's Day.

Writing a personal ad can be great fun. Before turning your students loose on this assignment, be sure to read the questions out loud and go over the list of vocabulary words. Then demonstrate how the ideas and vocabulary words can be brought together into an ad. Students who finish early may earn extra credit for doing a collage. (This option also keeps them busy and quiet while the other students complete the assignment.)

The radio ad activity offers a welcome alternative to worksheets and appeals to students with auditory learning styles. Have students do this assignment in pairs or small teams. Begin by developing a script with everyone giving input. Then try to show what a "homemade" (classroom-made) radio ad sounds like by making one of your own.

Two radio script types and formats are shown. The first is built around a short story that illustrates the need for a product. It portrays a person with a problem, and a solution to the problem: the product. The second is a public service announcement (PSA) designed to persuade listeners to join a cause.*

Allow students to hold two rehearsals before making their final recording: one without the sound equipment, and the other a full "dress rehearsal" using the sound equipment in the location where the final recording will be made (for example, the library or media center). The dress rehearsal will help everyone get accustomed to using the equipment, coordinating their voices, and working within the constraints of the recording room. Bypassing the dress rehearsal may result in disappointing tape productions. Students may also want to make a "practice tape" before making their final tape.

● ●

ABOUT THE HANDOUT FOR THIS LESSON

The Television Script form (page 66) is simply a lined page your students can use when writing their scripts. It will help them to follow the proper format. Have plenty of copies available for students whose scripts run longer than a single page.

● ●

---

* For more about public service announcements and other forms of social action, see *The Kid's Guide to Social Action* (Minneapolis: Free Spirit Publishing, 1991). *Expanding Work Opportunities: Working in Community Service* is a book I wrote for grades 6 through 10 that includes several ideas for service projects. For more information, write to Educational Design, 47 W. 13th, New York, NY 10011.

Poetry

- Students expand their definition of and appreciation for poetry—and the great variety possible in poetic forms of writing—by addressing the question, "What is poetry?" They explore the use of visual and sensuous language, rhythms, and varied word structures. They learn how to make up words or combine them to form new poetic images.

- As advertising was used in the previous lesson, poetry is used here to help students become more expressive in their choice of words. The activities encourage them to reach for more complex, descriptive, and vivid phrases. This comes together in a 13-line poem they write about a friend, using a prescribed set of rules.

- The PoemBuilder game—originally written as an algorithm for a software program—provides a fun and challenging enrichment activity. By operating this "poetry program" manually (using paper and pencil), students see how random qualities are related to creativity and how structure can emerge from play and chaos. The structure is strengthened when students revise their poems. The act of revising takes on new purpose. PoemBuilder also reinforces the skills needed to follow directions.

This section is really an introductory "taste" of poetry as a whole. Its effectiveness depends in large part on *your* attitude. If you feel uneasy about teaching poetry, or if you fear that your students will automatically reject poetry writing assignments, this lesson will be more of a struggle for everyone. In fact, most students in most classes express little or no interest when first invited to write poetry. I guarantee that this can change! Instead of assuming that your students will resist learning about poetry, try assuming that everyone can find some fun in writing one or two different forms of poetry. That way, you won't torpedo this lesson inadvertently.

Of course, if you really *hate* poetry, don't try to teach it. Skip this lesson or ask someone else to teach it for you. On the other hand, if you enjoy poetry so much that you write it yourself, bring in a sample of your writing to share with the class.

● ●

ABOUT THE HANDOUTS FOR THIS LESSON

● 13-Line Poem Starters (page 67) accompanies the student activity titled People Poems in 13 Lucky Lines. I have made this a reproducible form in case your students want to do this activity more than once.

● The two PoemBuilder Word Lists (pages 68–69 and 70–71) and the PoemBuilder Chart (page 72) are given to students during the PoemBuilder game. Again, you may want to repeat this game during the year, and students may need fresh word lists and charts each time.

● ●

What Is Poetry?

Let your students get crazy when they answer this question. Encourage them to use actual sounds to describe sounds. For example: "How would you write the sound a frog makes? How about 'r-r-r-v-v-t-t-t'? Could a line of poetry include sounds as well as descriptions of sounds? Could it go like this: 'The old frog r-r-r-v-v-t-t-t-ed and croaked away the night'?" Challenge your class to describe the sound of snow.

Introduce the idea that poetry lines are unlike paragraph lines. Show them how poets break lines to emphasize a single image, word, sound, or phrase. You may want to illustrate this with song lyrics.

Tips for Poem Writing Exercises #1 and #2

Exercise #1 helps students break free of the sentences-and-paragraphs writing habit. Explain that they may choose to capitalize the beginning of each line, or not—it's up to them. You may want to bring in a poem by e. e. cummings to illustrate this point. Write student poems on the board and show how to revise and polish them. (Often, student poetry is too wordy and needs to be cut.)

Exercise #2 is a simple and foolproof way for creating Western-type haiku. Once again, help your students "cut the flab" and get to the main idea. You may want to extend this lesson by holding a 6-Line Poem Contest.

About PoemBuilder

Some teachers use PoemBuilder as their introductory activity. Students enjoy playing the game and discovering that they really *can* write good poems.

After students complete their first rough drafts, help them to evaluate their words and lines. Ask them to circle the parts they like best. If there are words and/or lines they're not satisfied with, suggest that they go back to their word lists to find new words and phrases. In a typical six-line PoemBuilder poem, two lines will contain very usable poetry and two will have to be completely rewritten. Almost all of the lines will require some deletions, additions, and re-ordering of words and phrases.

The following poems were written by students with special needs using PoemBuilder. The students received a bit of help in revising and polishing their final poems.

NITE AND DAY

Nite and day
girl you make me feel good.
Baby
that serious smile on your face
makes the colorful rainbow come out and peek.

You're just like a piece of chocolate:
nice, creamy, and smooth.
Baby
You form this feeling in my heart
that makes me nutty nite and day!

PIZZA

Human-made food!

Cheerful
it tastes Godly!

Hot and soft pizza
makes your mouth water.

A real nose treat!

SILVER EAGLE

(a poem about a car)

It's a joyful car
with gas to burn;
A human-made, smooth Nissan
flying down the road.

The head person makes a hot, smooth machine.

Speeding, automatic, Silver Eagle
crashes through the old styles.

MY MAN BILL

Wild man Bill moves things smoothly.

Singing many different songs
while working,

That's my wild man for you.

As you work with your students, suggest ways to make their poems more meaningful, as illustrated in the following before-and-after samples:

Original PoemBuilder

Susaning lips
Cherry
Woman, soft-sounding natural rich
beautiful good scent hot
sweet red smile
makes us laugh

Final Version

Susan helps people.
She is a woman, soft-sounding.
Natural and rich with friends
your sweet, cherry red smile
makes me laugh.

Notice that some of the poetic devices (like adding "-ing" to the name Susan) were dropped in the final version. The word "cherry" was moved to another line because it fit the concept of a smile. The student was helped to change the first line when I asked, "What is it you most like about Susan?" I also asked, "What is Susan rich in besides money?"

Use questions and suggestions to help your students turn their PoemBuilder drafts into good poems. Don't hesitate to suggest that they cut some words, recombine others, and add new ones. That's what rewriting is all about.

My students enjoy PoemBuilder because it gives them a way to get started writing. That's our mission as teachers: giving our students a way to get started, then leading them to see the many possible forms of expression available to them—including poetry.

Ending the Lesson

The following techniques have proved very useful to me in introducing and teaching poetry. They can turn this lesson into a memorable, even celebratory experience for you and your students.

- Publish a poetry magazine, using student and staff contributions. Hold a contest to determine the title of the magazine. Invite an artistic student to create the cover (or hold another contest). Include photographs of the poets whose work appears in the magazine.

- Invite a local poet to visit your class and read his or her poems. If you need help finding poets, check with local bookstores, colleges or universities, or community education resources.

- Have a poetry reading party.

- Sponsor a poetry contest with judges and prizes, or put your students in touch with existing contests. Ask librarians and other teachers for information about contests.

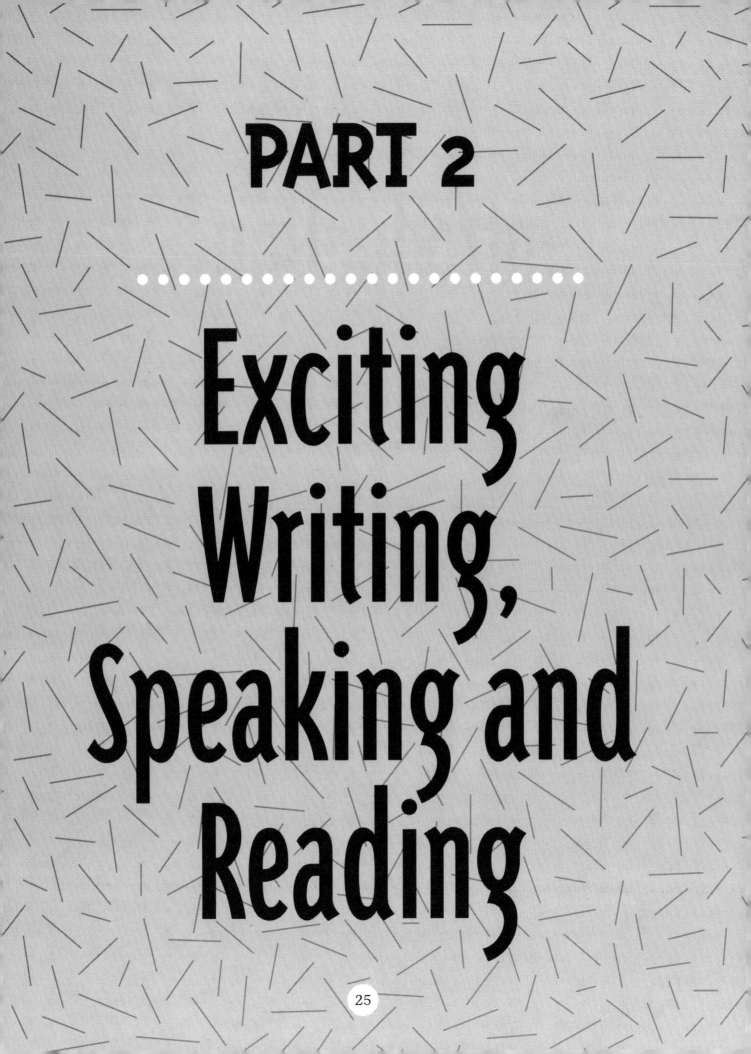

PART 2

Exciting Writing, Speaking and Reading

Introduction

art 2 of *Exciting Writing, Successful Speaking* focuses on public speaking and drama. For many students, giving a speech is frightening, and drama is intimidating. These lessons make both accessible and fun.

As you will discover, many of the activities in Part 1 have a natural carry-over to Part 2. Experience gained from the poetry lesson of Part 1 will enhance the public speaking lesson of Part 2. The radio and TV scripts completed in the advertising lesson of Part 1 lead to the theater games and script writing lesson of Part 2. Power Writing and 4-Step Writing, both learned in Part 1, make all of the writing activities in Part 2 easier and more "doable." The public speaking and theater games lessons also include simple activities that emphasize nonverbal forms of communication.

Part 2 also includes three additional lessons students enjoy. The Home Assignment illustrates how the process of writing is remarkably similar to other creative "constructions." Because this assignment is a thorough review of 4-Step Writing, it begins Part 2. In Publishing a Classroom Newsletter, students create a real publication from beginning to end. Finally, Imaginative Literature and Story Assignments enhance students' understanding of characterization, plot, and setting to make reading more meaningful and pleasurable.

Home Assignment

- The Home Assignment reviews and reinforces the basic 4-Step Writing process students learned in Part 1. Students remember or "build" a favorite house on a foundation of paragraphs.

- Students write a three-paragraph essay. Special emphasis is placed on the opening and closing sentences for each paragraph.

Drawing floor plans (top views of structures) and elevations (front or side views) may be new to some students. You may wish to illustrate how one's bedroom can be drawn in a floor plan format showing walls, windows, doors, furniture, etc. You might explain that drawing a floor plan is like taking the roof off of a house, looking straight down, and drawing what you see. An elevation might best be illustrated by drawing the front, back, or one side of the school.

The 4-Step Writing process taught in Part 1 has been expanded for this assignment. If the length and the emphasis on opening and closing sentences are new to your students, you may want to spend some classroom time on these skills prior to introducing this activity.

This lesson can also serve as an introduction to learning and working styles.

● ●

ABOUT THE HANDOUT FOR THIS LESSON

The 4-Step Writing Planning and Scoring Sheets
introduced in Part 1 have been revised for the Home
Assignment in Part 2 (pages 73–74). They now include
a special emphasis on opening and closing sentences.

● ●

Public Speaking

- Students practice nonverbal and verbal forms of communication including gestures, voice inflections, and articulation.

- They learn about and practice public speaking skills including approaching the podium, making eye contact, and using good posture.

- They learn how to organize a formal prepared speech, starting with a standard outline and adding gestures, props, and visual displays.

Believe it or not, your students will really enjoy most of these assignments. At first they may belly-ache, but soon they will be actively involved in the game-like warm-up activities. (The tongue twisters are always fun and popular.) As they become more engaged and used to performing, they move willingly into public speaking.

In my classes, we use the Speaker Rating Form (see page 75) to evaluate student performances. Each student gets a copy of the rating form. Each speaker is rated by three people:

- the teacher,

- himself or herself, and

- one other student the speaker chooses to evaluate his or her speech.

Following the speech, all students study the form and think about how they would fill it out for the speaker, but only three people (the teacher, the speaker, and the student chosen by the speaker) actually complete their forms. The final grade is a combination of the three evaluations, with each given equal weight. (If you find that speakers rate themselves lower than you or their classmates do, be sure to correct for this in the final grading.)

I begin each evaluation by asking the class, "What did you like best about the speech you just heard?" Then I go down the items on the Speaker Rating Form and ask student volunteers to share their ratings.

Two instructions help to keep student criticism on track and constructive. First, I remind everyone that it is better to be generous because eventually they will be in the "hot spot" themselves. Second, if they give anyone a rating of less than 3 (average), they must cite a reason with a positive rather than negative emphasis. For example, "I think the speaker had bad posture" is not acceptable; "I would have given a 4 instead of a 3 if the speaker had stood up straight" is acceptable. Even better is "I have a problem standing up straight when I speak, too, so I understand." If your group does not give feedback in a positive and sensitive way, have them write their comments rather than say them. Examine them and pass on to the speaker only those that are appropriate and helpful. In my classes, students give out a lot of 4's and 5's.

A good way to introduce the section on prepared speeches is to deliver a speech yourself. In fact, it's wise to model any and all activities in this lesson, depending on your students' abilities and willingness to try new things on their own.

● ●

ABOUT THE HANDOUT FOR THIS LESSON

The Speaker Rating Form (page 75) is an easy-to-use tool for evaluating student speeches.

● ●

Theater Games and Script Writing

- Drama and script writing work extends the skills and knowledge developed in previous lessons on advertising writing and public speaking. It also enhances students' overall writing skills.

- The lesson begins with theater games. Similar to charades, these are used as warm-ups and training exercises in acting classes. Like previous work in gesture, theater games require students to "show" or act out a message. Some games stress visual concentration; others emphasize trust, as in ensemble work. Still other games call upon the students' problem solving abilities as they improvise solutions for various problems or situations. This may sound daunting at first, but it is very natural and easy to do.

- The importance of "showing" rather than telling in dramatic work strengthens students' writing abilities by reinforcing the use of active, demonstrative communication techniques.

- Learning to write scripts sharpens students' observational powers as they strive to create realistic and credible dialogue. Learning how to organize an introduction and conclusion to a dramatic conflict or scene develops their skills in plot and character analysis. Personal experience with dramatic language makes it easier to understand plots and characters in literature. Familiarity with acting and script writing techniques encourages the inclusion of dialogue and quotations in reports, journals, and creative writing.

If your students have not yet experienced reading skits aloud, you may want to spend some time on this before beginning the drama lesson.

Theater Games

Playful and freeing, these games are fun for everyone, including you, so be sure to participate. There is only one key to success: Believe in them. If you are hesitant or doubtful, try teaming with the drama teacher or a drama student for the first few games.

The best and simplest approach is to follow the rules and suggestions provided for each game. The hints provided here help you to adapt a game when necessary. The follow-up questions are good for debriefing and reinforcing what has been learned.

You may choose to play the games as a class or break up into smaller groups. Either way, you should begin by reading the directions to the students, then illustrating for them or brainstorming with them ideas for playing or acting out each game.

Grocery Bag

Hints

If students have difficulty demonstrating and guessing the foods being eaten, write a list of foods on the board and work from this. Then the audience only has to match the actor's demonstration to the foods on the list. This cuts down the number of wrong guesses.

Remind the actors to respect the grocery bag. They must reach over the top and into the bag, not through it.

Follow-Up Questions

- *Was the performance believable?*

- *What was the best clue the actor gave?*

- *How could the actor have shown more detail when eating the food?*

- (For audience members): *How would you act out this situation differently? Show us....*

- (For the actor): *Would you like to try again?*

Chores

Hints

If students have difficulty acting out or interpreting chores, work from a fixed list on the board. Ask the actor to show details like putting on special clothing, opening and closing drawers, starting up machinery (lawnmower, vacuum cleaner), and so on.

Follow-Up Questions

● *Was the performance believable?*

● *What was the best clue the actor gave?*

● *How could the actor have shown more detail?*

● *How could the chore have been done differently?*

● (For audience members): *How would you act out this situation differently? Show us....*

● (For the actor): *Would you like to try again?*

Mirror, Mirror on the Wall...

Follow-Up Questions

● *What is eye contact?*

● *What is concentration?*

● *Why is it important to make eye contact when you are meeting another person for the first time?*

● *Why is knowing how to concentrate important? What is concentration good for?*

Seeing Eye

Follow-Up Questions

● *Do you know anyone who is blind or visually impaired?*

● *Have you ever been surprised by the things blind people can do? (Examples: certain jobs, sports, etc.)*

● *How did you treat your partner when you were "blind"? When your partner was "blind"?*

● *Did you feel uncomfortable at any time during this game? Talk about it.*

Walk That Walk

Hints

There is an alternative form of this game you may want to consider: Everyone lines up along one side of the room. One step at a time, they start crossing to the other side as you read the list of possible walks on pages 103–104 of the student book. For example. you might say, "Start walking.... Suddenly, you are barefoot walking across hot pavement..." (pause) "...very old and walking with a cane"...(pause)...and so on. The game becomes a version of Simon Says, except that everyone follows Simon's instructions at the same time. It's fun for students to "switch gears" suddenly and watch one another take on the new roles. It's interesting for you to see which student(s) are the most imitated.

Follow-Up Questions

- *What clues told you which type of walk each actor was performing?*

- *Was the performance believable?*

- *What was the best clue the actor gave?*

- *How could the actor have shown more detail when walking the walk?*

- (For audience members): *How would you do this walk differently? Show us....*

- (For the actor): *Would you like to try again?*

Tardy!

Follow-Up Questions

- *What clues told you which type of student each actor was portraying?*

- *Which type of student are you?*

- *Do you think that most people are able to act in only one way, or can we act in other ways?*

- *Do you act differently around different teachers?*

- *How would you want to act around a boss?*

- *Which way of acting makes your life easier?*

- *Did the person playing the teacher's role do it realistically?*

- *Can role playing another person help you to better understand him or her? Explain.*

Script Writing

My students take great delight in writing scripts. I have found that this usually works best when I let them work in twos and threes.

The activities in this section are designed to guide students in identifying and articulating a character's goals and obstacles. When a person's goal comes up against an obstacle, the result is dramatic conflict. Some students may view such conflict holistically, without breaking it down into its two parts—goals and obstacles. Keeping them separate, as I have done here, ensures that the scene does not develop too quickly or change too abruptly.

As you read your students' scripts, watch for these common traps, dilemmas, and mistakes:

- Some students write scripts with little or no conflict. They get so involved in writing dialogue that they forget to give it a purpose. For example, one student wrote a scene with this sequence: Student asks for car keys; parents say that student must first study and bring up grades; student agrees and makes smart-alec remark; the end. I suggested to the writer that he "punch up" the scene by adding another conflict. What if the student has promised to help clean up after a party his parents are giving, in exchange for the use of the family car? This sounds great until our character realizes that the party happens on the same night he wants to borrow the car. Now the student must wade through a more elaborate and more serious conflict.

- Some students write scripts with exaggerated conflicts. You can get around this by suggesting that it would be too difficult to stage or present in class. Brainstorm a toned-down version of the conflict.

- Many students have trouble with endings. Often they simply stop the dialogue or tack on a trite ending. For example, returning to the sequence about the car described above, the student might suddenly interject a phone call from a friend who offers to give the character a ride. Suggest that new characters and new plot devices cannot be brought in suddenly at the end. If the phone call is to be used, it should be introduced near the beginning (for example, the friend calls to ask for a ride) and reintroduced at the end (the friend calls back with news of a ride that has been found). Last-minute surprises almost always seem contrived.

- Students also have problems making plot and scene changes. Encourage the use of a narrator to perform this function. A narrator can give background details at the beginning, notify the audience of changes in time or scenery, and even make special sound effects.

The activities in this lesson should help students avoid most of these problem areas. Before staging the plays, look them over and offer feedback on the rough draft. Suggest new angles, new lines, new conflicts, and then ask for a final draft.

Finish this lesson by having students perform their skits for the class—or, better yet, invite another class in after the skits have been rehearsed. You might also consider a play writing contest, with the winning scripts acted out by a local drama group, class, or club. Alternatives to live performances might include videotaping for later showings.

You might choose to extend this lesson with one of the drama appreciation activities on pages 116–118 of the student book. Once your students are experienced playwrights, they will enjoy using their new knowledge to analyze and critique the work of others.

Publishing a Classroom Newsletter

- Planning, creating, and publishing a classroom newsletter draws on many of the skills learned so far in *Exciting Writing:* list writing (for brainstorming article ideas), 4-Step Writing (in a simplified version), journal writing (journal entries are a possible source of article ideas and even of articles themselves), advertising writing (if your newsletter includes ads), poetry writing and the PoemBuilder (if your newsletter includes student poems), even script writing (if your newsletter includes brief scenes or scripts).

- A classroom newsletter teaches cooperation and responsibility, since a publication cannot go to press until all the stories are in.

- As a natural part of the process, students gain valuable practice in several skills including interviewing, organizing information, using proper punctuation, and proofreading their writing.

- Students develop self-esteem when they see their peers reading and appreciating their stories.

This lesson describes a proven, practical, step-by-step process for planning and publishing a classroom newsletter. I use it with my regular students and special education students alike, and it works equally well in both settings. All kinds of students accept the assignments with enthusiasm and energy; the results usually include a lot of hustle-and-bustle during and pride afterward.

Our classroom newsletters are really literary publications containing newsletter-type articles, survey results, poems, and short fantasy stories. They are rarely "newsworthy" in the traditional sense, although we occasionally deal with school news. Mostly I let my students write about topics that interest them. I blend my traditional role as writing teacher and coach with a new role as editor, making assignments and coaching the "reporters."

We begin by nominating lead writers. I choose my two best writers from this group to write the lead stories for the front page. It's important to recognize that "best" doesn't always mean the obvious. Sometimes the "best" writers are those who may not write very well but who have a lot of imagination and creativity. Or the "best" writers might be those who have an especially good grasp of the theme or a personal experience or insight worth sharing. Or the "best" writers might be those who are seldom the "best" at anything, and who might rise to the challenge if you offer it to them. As the editor, you can help any and all of your students with their writing—including your lead writers.

The lead stories are on assigned topics that usually cover general school news (upcoming dances, theme for the year, school problems, etc.), require some research, and are long enough to take up two columns. The other students write shorter pieces, typically about cars, other teachers, clothes, records, romance, hobbies, local stores, poetry, etc. The point is for *everyone* to contribute *something*. This is a class effort.

When students want to interview another student or faculty member, they are required to submit their questions to me first. I help them to eliminate inappropriate or too-personal questions and supply ideas for more probing questions when needed. For my special education students who are interviewing teachers, I develop a questionnaire form, with blank spaces for writing, and suggest that they ask the teachers to write their answers on the form. When they return with the information, I help them organize it into a story. All of my students, at all ability levels, receive assistance in organizing their thoughts. I am an active editor! As a result, all of the pieces represent a collaboration between teacher-editor and student-author—just like in the real world.

Because students know that their work will be read by others, they are more than willing to be edited and to revise their writing. (I know that sounds hard to believe, but it's true.) They are asked to approve the final edits suggested by the editor (teacher), and they proof the galleys.

Producing a classroom newsletter usually takes about two to three weeks from beginning to end. I have found that if I do most of the word processing and desktop publishing myself, it can be completed in two weeks. Depending on how many computers you have available, all or most of the stories can be word processed by the students themselves, saving time and work for you.

You may want to involve your students in the desktop publishing stages—choosing the graphics, laying out the pages, fitting the copy and graphics into the layouts, designing headlines, etc. However, you should be aware that this will probably add several days to the project. It all depends on how familiar your students are with desktop publishing. If you have to train them, this will take more time, and you will also need to wait for them to complete the work. Of course, once they know what they are doing, it will take *less* time to produce future classroom newsletters because production responsibilities will be shared among several people.

Following is a description of the sequence of events I use with my students. Adapt this process to your own situation. You may find, for example, that you can have your students do more of the editing, word processing, and desktop publishing work.

1. Several possible lead writers are nominated by the class, and I choose two from this group.

2. The editorial policy is explained. For example: "We are writing to express our thoughts and to inform. We are not writing to criticize people, policies, or places. We can, however, share our ideas about problems and propose solutions."

3. The number of copies to be published and their distribution are determined. For example, we usually run off 60-70 copies, allowing 10 copies each (classroom sets) for several other teachers as well as samples for administrators, parents, and student writers.

4. Article topics are chosen from the Newsletter Planning Chart (see pages 76–77). You may decide to limit your students' choices to a single theme or section of the worksheet. For example, you may want to devote an issue to "Special Helpers" and ask your students to write about people from outside the class, such as custodians, secretaries, school counselors, teaching assistants, and coaches. You might assign (or suggest) a theme for the lead writers. This could be a school problem, a seasonal topic, or a question confronting today's youth and their families. The lead articles usually go on the front page of the newsletter.

5. Students are given individual help from beginning to end. For example, my students first meet with me to outline their strategy for gathering information. I might help them to develop their questions.

After they have finished gathering information (doing research, interviewing, surveying), we strategize further about ways to organize the information. This is a "prewriting" step. Finally, each student receives editing assistance from me on the first draft.

6. The rough drafts are edited and revised.

7. The final drafts are entered into the computer. If your class has limited access to computers or your students have limited keyboarding/computer skills, consider doing the data entry yourself, recruit a volunteer, or find a friendly business class teacher.

8. Students are invited to select the art for their articles. Ideally, they will be able to choose clip art from a computer program and modify it with a graphics program. Students enjoy finding, manipulating, and creating art and fancy titles. If you go this route, plan on an extra day or two for demonstrating the process and letting students practice before finalizing their art. If you don't have access to clip art and graphics programs, student art may be computer scanned or pasted directly onto the galleys.

9. The final art and articles are assembled with a desktop publishing program. The proof issue is created and copies are given to the writers to proof before printing. (You might also ask another teacher to proofread the newsletter.)

    NOTE: You may want to follow a simpler process. Instead of desktop publishing, just use a word processor or even a typewriter to output the text in columns. Allow space for some art work to be pasted in later. There are many books of copyright-free clip art available, as well as decorative tape that can be applied directly to the final output. Ask any journalism or drafting teacher for ideas.

10. The proof is corrected, printed, and sent to a district print shop. We typically run about 65 copies of a two- to four-page newsletter.

11. The newsletter is distributed. The first copies go to the student writers, who discuss the feeling of being published. They are asked to read all of the articles and think about what they would like to write about next time. Afterward, the remaining copies are hand-delivered to teachers selected by the students, and to school administrators.

My students enjoy distributing their publication and meeting their readers. They also enjoy reading and re-reading the newsletter. Many report keeping their newsletters for several years.

You might kick off your first newsletter with a visit to a local newspaper, or invite a reporter or editor in to talk to your class.

●●●●●●●●●●●●●●●●●●●●●●●●●●●●●●●●●●●●●●

ABOUT THE HANDOUT FOR THIS LESSON

The Newsletter Planning Chart (pages 76–77) helps students identify their areas of interest and decide what articles they might want to write. It is included here because you may want to re-use it for subsequent newsletter projects.

●●●●●●●●●●●●●●●●●●●●●●●●●●●●●●●●●●●●●●

Imaginative Literature and Story Assignments

- In this lesson, students build insight into characterization, setting, and plot.

- They practice imagining details, which makes their own writing more lively, colorful, and interesting.

- In order to complete these assignments, students must project themselves into characters' lives, settings, and plots. They might be asked to list the TV programs a main character would watch, guess the grades a character might earn in school, plan what to bring if they were to enter a story setting, or write a cartoon strip showing the sequence, plot, or theme of a story.

- These activities link the empathy students practiced in the Theater Games lesson with the empathy needed to read literature on more than a surface level.

Many of the activities and techniques in this section can be used with short stories, magazine articles, and newspaper articles as well as with plays, books, movies, and even cartoons. In my experience, it works best to start with a short story, then proceed to a movie on video, and finally focus on a longer reading assignment. Have students complete some of the assignments with partners; it's more fun, and two heads are sometimes better than one when it comes to imagining what a fictional character might say or do.

Before introducing an assignment, you might ask questions like the following to start students thinking about characterization, setting, and plot:

Character analysis:

● *What two or three words best describe the kind of person (character's name) is?*

Examining the setting:

● *How would your life change if you found yourself living where this story takes place?*

Plotting the main events:

● *Using only four to six words or phrases, tell what happens in the story.*

Spend some time bridging from story to activity, so the students remember to concentrate on the main character's point of view instead of giving their own. For example, you might introduce the Dating Service activity with questions like the following:

● *(Student's name), you said earlier that you felt the main character was selfish. Would you want to go on a date with him or her?*

● *From what you know about the character, is he or she the kind of person who would go to a dating service?*

● *What kind of person would the main character want to go out with? What qualities or characteristics would be important to him or her?*

PART 3

Exciting Reporting

Introduction

n Part 3 of *Exciting Writing, Successful Speaking*, students apply the writing and speaking skills they learned in parts 1 and 2 to longer and more extensive projects. They begin by creating a survey—collecting data, writing a report on the survey, and sharing the information orally with the class. Next, they learn a simplified process for creating book reports—both written and oral—that involves the use of a Reading Journal. Following this, they learn a comprehensive process for writing more detailed reports. They begin with a topic familiar to them: their own history. In preparing their autobiographies, they learn the basic steps used to prepare any report of substance: research and note-taking, organizing information and ideas, outlining, expanding the outline into a first draft, writing the final draft, and compiling a basic bibliography.

In the final part of this lesson, students write a longer report on a topic of their choosing. They are encouraged to gather information not just from books and periodicals, but also through personal interviews and telephone surveys. Planning sheets help track their efforts and may be used in grading their work.

There are many different ways to implement long-term projects. For example, some teachers give their students from one to three weeks to complete a major report. During this period, the students are given daily instruction on the different aspects of a research paper, and daily opportunities to work on their papers in class. While this type of step-by-step instruction is helpful for some students, others fail to develop important skills that long-term reports are supposed to teach—such as planning and budgeting one's time in order to complete the report by the deadline.

I prefer a somewhat different approach. Generally, I give my students from two to four weeks to complete a long-term report, and we work on them in class about two days out of the week. However, I expect my students to turn in some kind of project at the end of each week—perhaps their book log, reference note cards, outline, or first draft, depending on where we are in the process. This way, my students experience having to meet a deadline each week as well as a final deadline. They get a "nudge" and some support from me at least once a week, which helps them to stay on track and budget their time appropriately. Meanwhile, I can identify early those students who have problems in this area and make sure that the final deadline doesn't take them by surprise. I also give my students points or partial grades each week, rather than an all-or-nothing grade when the report is due.

I have found that many students need help in the following four skill areas:

1. understanding how an outline is formatted,

2. preparing an outline,

3. translating the notes from their reference cards and deciding where to fit them into the outline, and

4. compiling bibliographies.

If your students will have access to computer references and data bases (e.g., CD-ROM) when preparing their reports, they may need help using these as well.

You may want to illustrate these skill areas with examples before assigning a long-term report. Start with a class presentation (perhaps using overheads of some of the activities found in the student section). Some students will need to work with you on an individual or project level.

Doing a Survey

- Students learn how to develop survey questions which generate quantifiable results.

- Working in small groups, they choose a survey topic and plan how to collect data, prepare a report, and share their results.

- Students write a report using an established outline.

We live in a world of surveys. It seems as if we are always being asked to give our opinions about politicians (presidents, members of Congress), legislation (national, state, and local laws), new products (movies, soft drinks, cars), attitudes toward new policies (year-long schools), or our values concerning certain principles and beliefs (sex education, family values, leisure attitudes, racism). Survey results reported on the news can sway public opinion—and perhaps change the entire course of a nation.

Students often need to use survey skills to complete assignments in social studies, science, health, math, and English classes. Most students enjoy conducting surveys. The detailed steps in this assignment guide students through the web of designing, conducting, and reporting the results of a survey. Small teams of two to four students have worked best in my classes.

There are two critical areas you will want to monitor during this assignment. The first involves the creation of the survey questions. (Some people go to college to learn how to write good survey questions; your students will learn the basics from you.) The keys to a good survey question are *specificity* and *limited scope*. On their own, students tend to ask questions that are far too general ("Do you like the food here?") or too direct, begging an answer that is less than honest ("Do you take drugs?").

To help students evaluate their questions, ask:

- *Can your question be answered in more than one way? If it can, this will make it hard to interpret or compare your results.*

● *Could your question make somebody nervous or uncomfortable about answering?*

Demonstrate how to move a question from general to inferential. For example, "Do you like the cafeteria food?" will not yield useful results. But if students learn that their classmates are eating more frequently in the cafeteria, or recommending the food to others, or might even be willing to pay more for the food, it can be *inferred* that they are satisfied. So the question to ask might be "Do you eat in the cafeteria this year more, less, or about the same as last year?" or "Would you recommend the cafeteria to a visitor?" or "Would you be willing to pay twenty-five cents more a day to eat in the cafeteria?"—or all three.

Show how to move a question from too specific to inferential. To do this, students either need to form a hypothesis (something they think may be true and want to test) or develop an over-arching question that focuses the survey. This "big question" in turn suggests supporting questions which can be used to infer what respondents believe. For example, "Do you take drugs?" is not likely to generate honest answers; rather, it will force respondents into evasion or bravado. Better questions might include "Do you know anyone who has taken drugs?" (which takes the focus off of the respondent), "Do you think people your age take too many drugs?" (an indirect measure of frequency), and/or "Which drugs do you think are most widely used today?" From there, capture data with an open-ended question such as "What do you think needs to be done about drugs?" You may want to limit the response to a forced choice; for example: "a) have longer jail terms for drug dealers, b) legalize some drugs, c) teach people more of the real facts about drugs, d) pass stricter laws about drugs." This will determine if there is a consensus among survey respondents. Tip: The choices offered should be broad enough that respondents don't get stuck on specifics. "Have longer jail terms for drug dealers" is better than "Have 20-year mandatory jail terms for all drug dealers."

The second area to monitor involves the way students interpret their survey results or raw data. It is at this point that flawed questions reveal themselves with inconclusive results. Point out that most surveys contain some flawed questions because it isn't possible to second-guess everyone.

Many students will probably need help summarizing or tabulating totals. After they tabulate or count their survey data, perhaps you can figure the averages or percentages, or demonstrate for them how they can do this. As another alternative, enter their totals into a spreadsheet-charting soft-ware program that can turn the data into various graphs and charts automatically.

Next, your students will need to be coached on how to arrive at a sound conclusion, supported by the data. Sometimes one simply concludes that there is no consensus on a particular issue. Finally, your students may need help preparing their survey reports. All survey reports should be done in pencil or on a word processor for ease in editing.

How much time will this assignment take? Following the practice and completion of the student activities and worksheets, I generally allow two days of class time for planning and creating a final survey instrument. Students work in groups, and each student has an agreed-upon role. For example, one student will type the survey, and another will type the final report. They decide how many people each group member will interview and who will give an oral report to the class at the end.

I ask my students to conduct their surveys outside of class, as a homework assignment. If some students are too shy to do this, see if you can find another teacher who will let his or her students be surveyed during class time. After my students have conducted their surveys, I give them one day to tabulate or summarize their results, and another day to outline their report. A third day is set aside for completing the written report and practicing what to share in an oral report. You can use the oral report to reinforce skills learned in Part 2, Public Speaking. The survey assignment can also feed into a classroom newsletter as described in Part 2, Publishing a Classroom Newsletter. Use one issue of a newsletter to feature survey results.

Before you begin this unit, notify your administration that you will be teaching a unit on surveys. Ask your principal if he or she would like to review your students' survey topics or set any limits on the scope of the survey. For example, some of my students have asked to survey people about sensitive matters such as "Are you a member of a gang?" or "Have you ever had sex?" or "Have you ever been arrested?" These kinds of questions may not be appropriate, since they are loaded with peer pressure and are very personal. You might invite the principal to speak to your class, address the issue of surveying students about controversial topics, and suggest that sensitive and personal issues may not be proper subjects for a school survey. Clearing the ground on this issue first will prevent surprises later.

● ●

ABOUT THE HANDOUT FOR THIS LESSON

The Survey Report Form (pages 78–80) helps students organize their survey information and findings in preparation for writing a report.

● ●

Easy Book Reports and the Reading Journal

- Students follow a general outline for producing a book report. The outline is then re-used for an oral book report. These skills reinforce techniques learned in Part 2, Public Speaking. They also lead into outlining and recording techniques that will be used in the next section on research and report writing.

- Students learn how to use a reading journal to keep track of information they read about characters and plot.

Reading books and reporting on them offers a nice change of pace from regular classroom activities. The room gets suddenly quiet (unless you are in my room, where students bring in music tapes to play). Before doing oral book reports, you might want to consider reviewing the techniques presented in Part 2, Public Speaking.

Some teachers like to ease their classes into reporting about fiction by introducing the concepts with short stories, videotapes, or short magazine articles. This helps prepare students for tackling books of 100 pages or longer. When you begin with smaller reading assignments, you can concentrate on teaching the techniques of keeping a log, outlining, and public speaking.

I sometimes read stories out loud to my special education classes. Afterward, we discuss what might be entered in a reading journal, and students can copy the ideas they want to use in their journals.

● ●

ABOUT THE HANDOUTS FOR THIS LESSON

● The Reading Journal form (page 81) gives students an easy way to start and continue a reading journal. You may want to make several copies and keep them in a folder so students can take one whenever they need it.

● The Speaker Rating Form introduced in Part 2, Public Speaking, has been revised for the Oral Book Report in this lesson (page 82). It now includes rating categories specific to the book on which the student is reporting.

● ●

Writing a Short Report: The (Auto)Biography

- Students use a general life questionnaire to collect information about their own history or the history of another person. This information is then used to write a report about a life: an autobiography, if they are writing about themselves, or a biography, if they prefer to write about somebody else.

- Students begin by organizing their information into a report outline. Outlining skills are heavily emphasized in this introduction to report writing. This prepares students for the more challenging report writing assignment in the next lesson.

- Because they are writing about a familiar subject—their own life— students are free to concentrate on the specific techniques and overall process of preparing a report. Along the way, they learn and practice important skills needed for planning, drafting, revising, compiling bibliographies, and giving oral reports. The life story is a perfect vehicle for introducing the organizational skills needed to write a longer report or term paper.

Students enjoy writing about themselves. Almost all students with whom I have used this lesson have delighted in filling out the questionnaire.

In my experience, when assigning a report, it is better to specify a range of pages—for example, 2 to 5—than to mandate a specific number of pages. Requiring a specific length encourages "copy work" (as in copying pages from an encyclopedia) rather than promoting original writing. You will not have that problem here—when writing about themselves, most students exceed the number of pages they would ordinarily write—but it's worth keeping in mind.

Be sure to demonstrate the different techniques involved in outlining, and also the sequence of steps involved in report writing. Doing this now will pay off later, when your students tackle the final project in *Exciting Writing, Successful Speaking:* a longer, more heavily researched paper. The activity sheets included in that project will help students plan their work and target dates for completing the various steps.

As many students will discover, translating raw data from note cards into an outline is a challenging process requiring higher-order thinking skills such as synthesis. That is why I place so much emphasis on outlining and provide many examples. Students are able to observe how Jennifer, John, and Susan use outlines; Jennifer's example continues through later steps that involve turning an outline into a first draft.

Some students will only be able to copy the sample outline headings and supply their own details; others will come up with original schemes for outlining. Students who have great difficulty with synthesis and outlining may wish to follow a straight chronological outline, as in this example:

I. Childhood

    A. Where I lived

    B. Who I grew up with

    C. Who influenced me the most

II. Present times

    A. What I enjoy doing

    B. People who influence me today

    C. My interests: classes, sports, or hobbies I enjoy

III. My dreams for the future

    A. Where I hope to live

    B. What I hope to do for a living

    C. My dream for a happy life would be....

A few things need to be emphasized about using an outline as a basis for a longer report. Some students try to pack too many details into an outline. Point out that an outline by definition uses short sentences or phrases. Other students attempt to limit their final report to the language of the outline. Illustrate how outline notes suggest text and ideas which are then fleshed out in a rough draft. Be sure to call attention to the way Jennifer expanded her outline notes into a full-fledged draft. After your students study Jennifer's first paragraph, see what they can come up with for the second paragraph, using only the notes from Jennifer's outline.

ABOUT THE HANDOUTS FOR THIS LESSON

- The Steps and Schedule form (page 83) reinforces the report writing steps and helps students stay on task and on deadline. You may find it useful for all kinds of short reports you ask your students to write during the year.

- The Original Outline form (pages 84–85) provides practice in outlining skills and prepares students to write the first draft of their short report.

- The Speaker Rating Form introduced in Part 2, Public Speaking, and reintroduced in Part 3, Easy Book Reports and the Reading Journal, has been revised for the Short Report/(Auto)Biography in this lesson (page 86). It now includes a rating category specific to references.

Writing a Longer Report

- The final project in *Exciting Writing* builds on the organizing and writing skills developed in the previous lesson, Writing a Short Report: The (Auto)Biography.

- Several skills are added to the report-writing process which were not needed in the autobiography lesson. These include time management, choosing a topic that lends itself to collecting information in a reasonable amount of time, developing questions to guide research, selecting both written and human sources for information gathering, collecting information in an organized fashion (using note cards), and creating formal bibliographies.

I believe the key to success in this assignment lies in giving students the freedom to choose their own topics. This is important for several reasons. First, writing a longer report takes a great deal of time and effort, which requires a high degree of motivation. Picking one's own topic places the rocket of motivation on the launching pad. Second, students will feel more confident about solving research projects when they work with a topic that is familiar to them or interesting to them personally. They will be more at ease asking for help or information from a librarian or expert in the field. Third, it will be easier to synthesize a report from outline notes when one possesses some background on (or interest in) the topic to begin with. Finally, students take more pride in revising, making covers, and putting together bibliographies for topics they care about.

Because the topics your students choose may be wide-ranging, I recommend that you take an equally broad view of the sources and references they use. Try not to limit them to written or traditional library materials. Be creative and help your students to realize that our information society often makes useful information available in a variety of forms. Your students might gather research data by interviewing experts, reading brochures, and conducting surveys. They might use computer databases, CD-ROM, or multi-media sources. They might get in touch with their experts or conduct surveys via computer bulletin boards or networks. In fact, thinking about references creatively places your students—and you— in the mainstream of report writers today.

Before you begin this lesson, you may want to review the introduction to Part 3 on pages 46–47 of this Teacher's Guide, particularly the comments about helping students manage a long-term project across time. You probably will want to review the kinds of references available to your students in the library (or libraries) they will be using, including your school library or media center, your local public library, and perhaps any college or university libraries in your community that your students will be visiting during this project. For example: Are there books, brochures, magazines, or encyclopedias at your students' reading level(s)? Are there any special references, such as directories or catalogs of articles that have been collected about current social problems? Are there any special technologies (computers, faxes, modems) your students may use to access useful information? Consider people on your school's staff—counselors, social studies teachers, health teachers, support staff—as "field experts" and ask them if they are willing to be interviewed.

If possible, show samples of longer reports and term papers; this helps to place a vision of the final product in your students' minds. You may be able to obtain sample reports from other teachers. Better yet, start creating your own collection or classroom library of reports completed in your classes. Future students will be able to use these papers as references. Being selected for this special "library collection" could act as a final motivator for some students.

While the handouts included in the lesson guide students through the various steps of report writing, you will increase your students' understanding— and success—by demonstrating the steps a little at a time across several days. Pick topics your students are writing about and illustrate the steps on an overhead projector. Follow up by monitoring your student's progress and providing feedback. Otherwise, they might head off in the wrong direction and end up in a cul de sac from which there is no escape. Examples of how to demonstrate steps are given in the next section.

Two final comments, on length and grading: As noted in the Teacher Tips to Writing a Short Report: The (Auto)Biography, it is better to specify a range of pages than to mandate a specific number. For a longer report, you might require a range of 2-4 pages for junior high/middle school students, and 4-8 pages for high school students. These are *only* suggestions; use your own best judgment based on what you think your students can do. Naturally they should be aware that five handwritten pages do not equal five typewritten or word processed pages; if they write their papers by hand, they should be a bit longer.

●●●

ABOUT THE HANDOUTS FOR THIS LESSON

● The Time Management Worksheet (page 87) provides a written record of the due dates for the various tasks required to complete the report. Each task has been assigned a maximum number of points. You will need to determine how many points are required for a grade of A, B, or C and communicate this information to your students.

● The Topics, Questions, and References Approval Form (page 88) gives you an easy way to check on students' progress during the critical early stages of report writing. Hand out copies at the beginning of the lesson, along with the Time Management Worksheet. Make sure students understand that they must turn in their completed forms for your approval.

● The Special Reference Page (page 89) is an alternative to note cards for students who prefer more space for writing. Keep several copies on hand in a folder for students to use whenever they need them. To make reference pages stand out, copy them onto colored paper.

● The Report Outline form (pages 90–91) gives students a place to put the main elements of their report outline. You may want to collect these to check before the actual writing begins.

●●

Suggested Steps to Demonstrate

You may wish to demonstrate the following steps in the report writing process. This will give your students a chance to see what is expected of them and also to practice the skills required.

Formulating Questions

This first planning step can be tricky for some students. Show them that questions which are either too general or too narrow can make research difficult. It might also be helpful to illustrate how questions can be organized in terms of sequence or logic (one leading into another), chronology, importance, or difficulty.

Note Taking

Note taking may be a new skill for your students. If you make reference pages available on colored paper (see page 89 for a student handout), this gives the task a special emphasis, and colored paper makes it easier to locate reference notes among stacks of lined paper, class notes, and spiral binders.

Demonstrate the note taking process with a high-interest, easy-reading newspaper article. Show how to summarize the main facts in the first paragraph. Illustrate how to take notes by writing summary statements and copying facts and quotations accurately and completely. Then let students try doing the same with the remaining paragraphs. Ask them to show their work on the overhead projector.

Creative Researching

Ask students to find and use one reference from a list of non-book possibilities (examples: stores, magazines, brochures, experts [in-person or telephone interviews], informal surveys, computer multi-media, bulletin boards, CD-ROM, etc.). They must bring back the material they find on note cards to share with the class.

Outlining and Turning Outlines into Narratives and Drafts

Going from notes to an outline is the most difficult step in the report writing process, one that involves higher-order cognitive thinking skills (synthesis). To help your students grasp it, illustrate the following steps:

- grouping common ideas from various note cards
- developing headings for each group of ideas
- revising the groupings as needed.

Some students may write too much on an outline. What they are really doing is writing the first draft in outline form. The result is a congested narrative, not an outline. Encourage the use of short phrases or even single words as topics and subtopics.

Some students have the opposite problem: They write too little on their first draft. They literally copy their outline into a narrative format without expanding on their notes. In the student lesson for Part 3, Writing a Short Report: The (Auto)Biography, you'll find examples illustrating how to take notes and expand them into a first draft.

Writing the Introduction and Conclusion

In the student lesson for Part 3, Writing a Short Report: The (Auto)-Biography, you'll find examples illustrating these processes.

Preparing a Formal Bibliography

In the student lesson for Part 3, Writing a Short Report: The (Auto)-Biography, you'll find a basic introduction to preparing a rather informal bibliography. You may want to begin by reviewing it with your students. In this Longer Report project, your students will learn the skills and steps involved in preparing a more formal bibliography. Specific formats are provided for book references, magazine and newspaper article references, and other sources of information your students may use in preparing their reports.

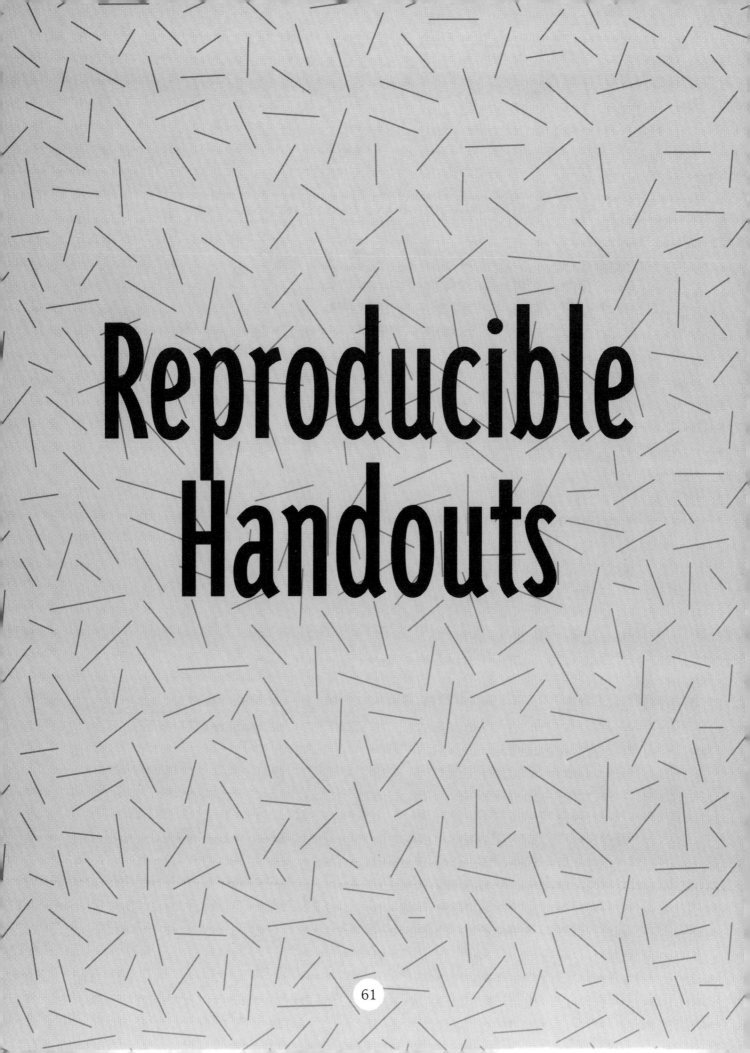

Reproducible Handouts

4-STEP WRITING PLANNING AND SCORING

For *Exciting Writing, Successful Speaking* Part 1

Name_____ Class_____ Period_____ Date_____

STEP 1: PREWRITING (BRAINSTORMING AND ORGANIZING IDEAS)

10 points possible **Your score:** _____

1. Choose a subject for your essay.
2. Power Write a list of words and ideas for your essay.

    (a) Write for 1-2 minutes. Keep your hand moving.

    (b) Try to come up with at least 8 ideas, since you'll be using at least 4 ideas per paragraph.

    5 points of the total 10 **Your score:** _____

3. Organize and revise your list. Try grouping your ideas into 2 or more lists, each list representing one paragraph.

    (a) Put your ideas in order.

    (b) If you group your ideas, have at least 4 in each group.

    (c) Add new ideas. Delete ideas you don't want to use.

    5 points of the total 10 **Your score:** _____

STEP 2: WRITING THE FIRST (ROUGH) DRAFT

5 points possible **Your score:** _____

4. Write as quickly as you can—without stopping. Follow these four rules:

    RULE #1: Ignore Spelling

    RULE #2: Skip Lines

    RULE #3: Keep Writing

    RULE #4: Don't Erase (just ~~cross out~~ words you don't want)

STEP 3: REVISING THE FIRST DRAFT AND WRITING THE SECOND DRAFT

5 points possible **Your score:** _____

5. Read your first draft out loud to yourself.

    (a) Add words, ideas, sentences; take out those you don't want anymore. Change things around.

    (b) Delete or change unclear sentences.

    (c) Make sure your first sentence grabs the reader. Use a question or summary statement.

6. Read your first draft out loud to a partner. Ask:

    (a) Which parts were most interesting?

    (b) Did I leave anything out? Was anything unclear?

    (c) Would you recommend changing anything?

7. Show the teacher your revised first draft. It should be marked up with your changes and ideas.

8. Write a clean copy of your second draft. Skip lines.

STEP 4: EDITING FOR THE FINAL DRAFT

5 points possible   **Your score:**_____

9. Edit your second draft with COPS. As you complete each step, check off the box.

Capitalization

☐ Capitalize the first word in each sentence.

☐ Capitalize all proper nouns.

Overall Appearance and Style (for the final draft)

☐ Keep your handwriting well-spaced and legible.

☐ Start with a clean piece of paper. Keep it neat (no smudges, tears, or extra marks)

☐ Use straight margins and indent the first sentence in each paragraph.

☐ Write a title on the top line.

Punctuation

☐ End each sentence with a . or ? or !

☐ Use commas when they are needed.

☐ Use complete sentences (subject and verb).

☐ Don't start sentences with "so," "but," "and," or "well."

Spelling

☐ Check words you often misspell.

☐ Circle any words you feel unsure about.

☐ Ask for help or look up the words you checked or circled.

10. Write your final draft in ink and turn it in.

Due:_____

4-STEP WRITING QUIZ

Name_____ Class_____ Period_____ Date_____

How much do you remember about 4-Step Writing? Answer as many questions as you can.
If you need help, check your 4-Step Writing handouts.

I am taking this test for the ☐ first time ☐ second time.

I am using ☐ my notes and handouts ☐ no notes or handouts.

1. What is Step 1?_____

   What three things does Step 1 include?

   1. _____

   2. _____

   3. _____

2. What is Step 2? _____

   What are the four rules of fast writing?

   RULE #1: _____

   RULE #2: _____

   RULE #3: _____

   RULE #4: _____

3. What is Step 3? _____

   You should read your first draft out loud to:

   1. _____

   2. _____

   Where should you mark your changes and corrections? _____

4. What is Step 4? _____

   What does **COPS** stand for?

   C: _____

   O: _____

   P: _____

   S: _____

5. Optional question: What part of 4-Step Writing has helped you to improve your writing
   the most? _____

   _____

   _____

JOURNAL

A book of my thoughts and writings by

_____

Journal Word Count Chart

Total Words Written															
over 150															
150															
120															
100															
95															
85															
75															
65															
55															
45															
35															
25															
15															
Write in the _date_, then the _month_															

TELEVISION SCRIPT

Audio Script
(Words, sounds, music)

Visual Script
(Pictures to shoot)

_____ _____

_____ _____

_____ _____

_____ _____

_____ _____

_____ _____

_____ _____

_____ _____

_____ _____

_____ _____

_____ _____

_____ _____

_____ _____

_____ _____

_____ _____

_____ _____

_____ _____

_____ _____

_____ _____

_____ _____

13-LINE POEM STARTERS

First Stanza

1. I am _____

2. I hear _____

3. I see _____

4. I am _____

Second Stanza

5. I pretend _____

6. I worry _____

7. I cry _____

8. I am _____

(Repeat line 1.)

Third Stanza

9. I say _____

10. I dream _____

11. I try to make a difference by _____

12. I hope _____

13. I am _____

(Repeat line 1.)

POEMBUILDER BEGINNING WORD LISTS

Check off the answers and write in the words from your completed PoemBuilder Survey. For example, if you checked "BIG" on the survey, check it here, too. Ignore the numbered words for now.

S: Senses Words

- ☐ BIG ¹large ²huge ³vast ⁴grand ⁵great ⁶big
- ☐ SMALL ¹tiny ²little ³pinch of ⁴slight ⁵small ⁶smallish
- ☐ HOT ¹boiling ²smoking ³warm ⁴glowing ⁵burning ⁶hot
- ☐ COLD ¹cool ²icy ³freezing ⁴chilly ⁵frosted ⁶cold
- ☐ NICE TO TOUCH ¹touchable ²cuddly ³smooth ⁴soft ⁵snug ⁶feels good
- ☐ NOT NICE TO TOUCH ¹painful ²sting ³ache ⁴hurting ⁵sore ⁶rough
- ☐ SMELLS GOOD ¹nice aroma ²perfumed ³good scent ⁴sweet-smelling ⁵smells good ⁶nose treat
- ☐ SMELLS STRONG OR BAD ¹foul ²stink ³nose-killing ⁴smelly ⁵bad-smelling ⁶stink up
- ☐ TASTES GOOD ¹tasty ²yummy ³lip-smacking ⁴rich-tasting ⁵delicious ⁶mouth treat
- ☐ TASTES STRONG OR BAD ¹stale ²sour ³bitter ⁴bad-tasting ⁵mouth hurt ⁶bitter pill
- ☐ LOUD ¹loud ²roar ³noisy ⁴blasting ⁵ear-hurting ⁶blaring
- ☐ QUIET ¹quiet ²soft-sounding ³hushed ⁴whisper-quiet ⁵faint ⁶quietly
- ☐ SOUNDS PRETTY ¹pretty-sounding ²ear heaven ³chime ⁴musical ⁵in tune with ⁶melodious
- ☐ SOUNDS AWFUL ¹noisy ²whining ³awful-sounding ⁴ear-grinding ⁵raspy ⁶sound-clashing

E: Emotions Words

- ☐ NATURAL ¹natural ²lifelike ³pure ⁴raw ⁵real ⁶growing
- ☐ ARTIFICIAL ¹human-made ²artificial ³built of ⁴built with ⁵made with tools ⁶unreal
- ☐ HAPPY ¹merry ²joyful ³glad feelings ⁴cheerful ⁵happy ⁶smile-maker
- ☐ SAD ¹sad ²unhappy ³crying ⁴gray-feeling ⁵frowning ⁶blue
- ☐ SERIOUS ¹serious ²thinker ³head person ⁴thinking ⁵heavy ⁶solemn
- ☐ FUNNY ¹humorous ²grin-maker ³tickles me ⁴laughing ⁵joking ⁶funny
- ☐ OLD ¹old ²wrinkled ³many years ⁴worn ⁵old-fashioned ⁶long ago
- ☐ NEW ¹shiny ²young ³future thoughts ⁴new ⁵modern ⁶just born
- ☐ COLORFUL ¹rainbowish ²colorful ³blended ⁴colors of ⁵beautiful ⁶colored
- ☐ ONE COLOR Write the color: _____

N: Naming Words

List the six names you wrote for your topic:

_____   _____

_____   _____

_____   _____

A: Action Words

List the six verbs or verb phrases you wrote for your topic:

_____   _____

_____   _____

_____   _____

C: Color Words

List the six colors you wrote for your topic:

_____   _____

_____   _____

_____   _____

POEMBUILDER ADVANCED WORD LISTS

(For writers who want to build their vocabulary)

Check off the answers and write in the words from your completed PoemBuilder Survey.

S: Senses Words

- ☐ BIG [1]enormous [2]gigantic [3]vast [4]huge [5]colossal [6]grand
- ☐ SMALL [1]tiny [2]miniature [3]petite [4]little [5]microscopic [6]small
- ☐ HOT [1]boiling [2]seething [3]smoking [4]scorching [5]glowing [6]hot
- ☐ COLD [1]frigid [2]chilly [3]icy [4]wintry [5]metallic [6]cold
- ☐ NICE TO TOUCH [1]caressable [2]luxurious [3]touchable [4]exciting [5]tactile [6]ticklish
- ☐ NOT NICE TO TOUCH [1]painful [2]sting [3]ache [4]hurting [5]sore [6]harsh
- ☐ SMELLS GOOD [1]aromatic [2]spicy [3]redolent [4]sweet-smelling [5]fragrant [6]ambrosial
- ☐ SMELLS STRONG OR BAD [1]foul [2]stench [3]stink [4]reek [5]rancid [6]smelly
- ☐ TASTES GOOD [1]savory [2]delicious [3]ambrosial [4]tasty [5]palatable [6]scrumptious
- ☐ TASTES STRONG OR BAD [1]foul [2]bitter [3]nauseating [4]tasteless [5]stale [6]sour
- ☐ LOUD [1]loud [2]sonic [3]boisterous [4]blaring [5]deafening [6]thunderous
- ☐ QUIET [1]muted [2]soft [3]hushed [4]faintly [5]whisperish [6]quiet
- ☐ SOUNDS PRETTY [1]resonant [2]symphonic [3]sonorous [4]melodious [5]harmonious [6]lyrical
- ☐ SOUNDS AWFUL [1]noisy [2]moaning [3]garbled [4]distorted [5]dissonant [6]screeching

E: Emotions Words

- ☐ NATURAL [1]natural [2]organic [3]native [4]raw [5]lifelike [6]genuine
- ☐ ARTIFICIAL [1]human-made [2]artificial [3]unnatural [4]manufactured [5]synthetic [6]built of
- ☐ HAPPY [1]exuberant [2]enchanted [3]delighted [4]inspiring [5]cheerful [6]joyful
- ☐ SAD [1]sorrowful [2]depressing [3]gloomy [4]dismal [5]mournful [6]oppressive
- ☐ SERIOUS [1]austere [2]official [3]ponderous [4]serious [5]earnest [6]solemn
- ☐ FUNNY [1]humorous [2]eccentric [3]comical [4]whimsical [5]ticklish [6]laughable
- ☐ OLD [1]ancient [2]seasoned [3]primordial [4]archaic [5]old [6]mature
- ☐ NEW [1]futuristic [2]newborn [3]modern [4]youthful [5]novel [6]progressive
- ☐ COLORFUL [1]chromatic [2]rainbowish [3]variegated [4]checkered [5]colorful [6]blended
- ☐ ONE COLOR Write the color: _____

N: Naming Words

List the six names you wrote for your topic:

_____   _____

_____   _____

_____   _____

A: Action Words

List the six verbs or verb phrases you wrote for your topic:

_____   _____

_____   _____

_____   _____

C: Color Words

List the six colors you wrote for your topic:

_____   _____

_____   _____

_____   _____

POEMBUILDER CHART

Lines of poetry Number of words per line	Words and Word Categories					
	Word 1	Word 2	Word 3	Word 4	Word 5	Word 6
1. ____	from Group__	from Group__	from Group__	from Group__	from Group__	from Group__
2. ____	from Group__	from Group__	from Group__	from Group__	from Group__	from Group__
3. ____	from Group__	from Group__	from Group__	from Group__	from Group__	from Group__
4. ____	from Group__	from Group__	from Group__	from Group__	from Group__	from Group__
5. ____	from Group__	from Group__	from Group__	from Group__	from Group__	from Group__
6. ____	from Group__	from Group__	from Group__	from Group__	from Group__	from Group__

Adding the C (Color) Words

Roll the die to select one or more words from your list. Put your C words near any words on your chart that you think they go with.

4-STEP WRITING PLANNING AND SCORING

For *Exciting Writing, Successful Speaking* Part 2

Name_____ Class_____ Period_____ Date_____

STEP 1: PREWRITING (BRAINSTORMING AND ORGANIZING IDEAS)

5 points possible   **Your score:** _____

1. Review your ideas from brainstorming.
2. Group your ideas into paragraphs—4 to 6 ideas per paragraph.
3. Number your ideas (first, second, third, etc.).

STEP 2: WRITING THE FIRST (ROUGH) DRAFT

10 points possible   **Your score:** _____

4. Write as quickly as you can. Leave extra lines before and after each paragraph for your opening and closing sentences. Follow these four rules:

    RULE #1: Ignore Spelling

    RULE #2: Skip Lines

    RULE #3: Keep Writing

    RULE #4: Don't Erase

    5 points of the total 10   **Your score:** _____

5. Write opening and closing sentences for each paragraph.

    5 points of the total 10   **Your score:** _____

STEP 3: REVISING THE FIRST DRAFT AND WRITING THE SECOND DRAFT

5 points possible   **Your score:** _____

6. Read your first draft out loud to yourself and make changes and improvements.
7. Read your first draft out loud to a partner and make changes and improvements.
8. If possible, read your essay out loud to your teacher and ask for feedback.
9. Write a clean copy of your second draft.

5 points possible **Your score:** _____

10. Edit your second draft with COPS. As you complete each step, check off the box.

    Capitalization

    ☐ Capitalize the first word in each sentence.

    ☐ Capitalize all proper nouns.

    Overall Appearance and Style (for the final draft)

    ☐ Keep your handwriting well-spaced and legible.

    ☐ Start with a clean piece of paper. Keep it neat (no smudges, tears, or extra marks)

    ☐ Use straight margins and indent the first sentence in each paragraph.

    ☐ Write a title on the top line.

    Punctuation

    ☐ End each sentence with a . or ? or !

    ☐ Use commas when they are needed.

    ☐ Use complete sentences (subject and verb).

    ☐ Don't start sentences with "so," "but," "and," or "well."

    Spelling

    ☐ Check words you often misspell.

    ☐ Circle any words you feel unsure about.

    ☐ Ask for help or look up the words.

11. Write your final draft in ink and turn it in.

Due:_____

SPEAKER RATING FORM

Speaker_____ Date_____

Evaluator: ☐ Teacher ☐ Myself ☐ Student: _____

	Excellent	Average		Needs Work
Good posture 5	4	3	2	1
Smiles 5	4	3	2	1
Eye contact 5	4	3	2	1
Clear and loud voice 5	4	3	2	1
Uses some gestures and voice variety 5	4	3	2	1
Approaches and leaves podium with dignity.......5	4	3	2	1
Speech was interesting......................................5	4	3	2	1
Speech was well-organized, went smoothly 5	4	3	2	1

What did you like best about the speech/speaker? _____

_____

_____

Overall rating: I'd give this person a 5   4   3   2   1

NEWSLETTER PLANNING CHART

Following are several ideas for newsletter articles. Look over this list with the other reporters and decide what you would like to work on. Check any story ideas you might be willing to write about. If you come up with ideas not included on the chart, write them in the spaces provided. Then narrow your choices down to the three that interest you the most. If you are one of the lead writers, your topic may not be listed here.

Theme Ideas

- ☐ What you think is the true meaning of an upcoming holiday or vacation period.
- ☐ Information about school changes—in classes, schedules, rules, buildings, classrooms, etc.
- ☐ Information about upcoming school events, sales, fund raisers, contests, etc.
- ☐ A description of a school problem and what students can do to help solve it.
- ☐ _____
- ☐ _____

Feature Stories

- ☐ Teacher Feature: Why you like a certain teacher.
- ☐ Special Helpers: Secretaries, PTA members, custodians, cooks, teachers' assistants, coaches, etc.
- ☐ Employers on and off campus.
- ☐ Guest speakers.
- ☐ The latest styles or trends in music, fashion, after-school recreation (examples: games), cars, etc.
- ☐ Information about clubs or groups you belong to.
- ☐ Your favorite class.
- ☐ How someone at school went out of his or her way to help you.
- ☐ _____
- ☐ _____

Special Stories

- ☐ Jobs for quick cash.
- ☐ Pet care or training.
- ☐ What you will do on an upcoming holiday—for example, Presidents' Day.
- ☐ Hunting or fishing stories.
- ☐ Crafts or hobbies.
- ☐ _____
- ☐ _____

Advice Columns

- [ ] The best place to buy pizza, fries, dessert, music, shoes, etc.
- [ ] Advice about upcoming holidays. Examples: what to give your boyfriend or girlfriend this Valentine's Day; how to keep from wasting spring break; how to make the most of a three-day weekend.
- [ ] Advice about teen problems like dating, getting around without a car, making friends, losing friends, feeling lonely, controlling your temper, grades, getting along with parents or teachers, etc.
- [ ] Tips for the new semester.
- [ ] _____
- [ ] _____

Creative Writing

- [ ] A poem on the issue theme or another subject of your choosing.
- [ ] A new caption/new dialogue for a cartoon you like—or draw a cartoon.
- [ ] An ad for a school event, sale, fund raiser, or contest.
- [ ] _____
- [ ] _____

Surveys and Reports

Do a survey and write a report on one of the following questions:

- [ ] How many bones have you broken in your lifetime?
- [ ] What is the longest you have gone without sleep?
- [ ] What is the highest temperature you have had?
- [ ] Who is the oldest person you know?
- [ ] Who has a birthday this month?
- [ ] Who has the best school attendance record?
- [ ] _____
- [ ] _____

My top 3 choices are:

1. _____
2. _____
3. _____

SURVEY REPORT

I. THE PURPOSE OF OUR SURVEY

    A. State your topic and why you chose it. Write your original prediction or hypothesis.

_____

_____

_____

_____

    B. Describe your general or main question.

_____

_____

_____

_____

II. THE METHOD WE USED FOR OUR SURVEY

    A. Describe who did what.

_____

_____

_____

_____

    B. Tell where the survey was done and who was surveyed.

_____

_____

_____

_____

    C. Describe how people reacted when you asked them to take part in your survey. Did they enjoy the survey?

_____

_____

_____

_____

D. Tell how many people you surveyed. (In some surveys, this is called the "N".) Then tell if you think your sample was large enough to represent most people's views.

_____

_____

_____

_____

III. TOTALS AND RESULTS

Write down each question. Figure the totals, averages, or percentages for each response. (Get help from your teacher if you need it to complete this step.)

_____

_____

_____

_____

_____

_____

_____

_____

_____

_____

_____

_____

_____

_____

_____

_____

IV. CONCLUSION AND RECOMMENDATIONS

A. Tell which survey result(s) supported your original hypothesis.

_____

_____

_____

_____

B. What surprised you about your survey totals? Which responses did you not predict very well?

_____

_____

_____

_____

_____

C. Can you make any recommendations based on your survey results? What does your survey seem to prove or suggest?

_____

_____

_____

_____

_____

Therefore, based on our survey, we recommend:

_____

_____

_____

_____

D. OPTIONAL: Use your report as an outline for an oral presentation. When planning your presentation, you may want to prepare handouts, blow-ups of your charts and graphs, or other materials to make your presentation more interesting and help your audience to see your results more clearly.

READING JOURNAL

Name_____ Class_____ Period____ Date_____

If you are reading a book:

Title: _____

Author: _____

Number of pages: _____

If you are reading a story from a magazine:

Story title: _____

Author: _____

Name of magazine: _____

Month:_____ Year:_____ Number of pages:_____

Date	Pages from____ to____	Describe what you read about. List the characters and tell what happened. Note anything else you want to remember.
____	____	_____
____	____	_____
____	____	_____
____	____	_____
____	____	_____
____	____	_____
____	____	_____
____	____	_____
____	____	_____
____	____	_____
____	____	_____
____	____	_____
____	____	_____
____	____	_____

Continue your journal for this book or story on another piece of lined paper. When you start another reading task, begin another Reading Journal page.

SPEAKER RATING FORM FOR ORAL BOOK REPORT

Speaker_____ Date_____

Evaluator: ☐ Teacher ☐ Myself ☐ Student: _____

	Excellent		Average		Needs Work
Did you speak with a convincing style?					
Good posture 5	4	3	2	I
Smiles 5	4	3	2	I
Eye contact 5	4	3	2	I
Clear voice, good volume...............................5	4	3	2	I
Shows excitement (uses some gestures and voice variety).......5	4	3	2	I
Did you fully describe the book?					
Describes characters......................................5	4	3	2	I
Describes what happened 5	4	3	2	I
Tells what was good and bad about the book 5	4	3	2	I
Reads a passage from the book......................5	4	3	2	I

What did you like best about the book? _____

_____

_____

_____

_____

_____

STEPS AND SCHEDULE

Step   Due by

1. _____   _____

2. _____   _____

3. _____   _____

4. _____   _____

5. _____   _____

6. _____   _____

7. _____   _____

8. _____   _____

                                                          Final Deadline

9. _____   _____

ORIGINAL OUTLINE

TIP: Fill in only as many lines, topics, and subtopics as you plan to write about. If you need more space, use more paper.

I. Introduction

_____

_____

_____

_____

_____

_____

_____

First Main Topic

II. _____

Subtopics

    A. _____

    B. _____

    C. _____

    D. _____

Second Main Topic

III. _____

Subtopics

    A. _____

    B. _____

    C. _____

    D. _____

Third Main Topic

IV. _____

Subtopics

    A. _____

    B. _____

    C. _____

    D. _____

(Other main topics and subtopics? Add more paper.)

X. Conclusion

_____

_____

_____

_____

_____

_____

_____

_____

_____

SPEAKER RATING FORM FOR SHORT REPORT

Speaker_____ Date_____

Evaluator: ☐ Teacher ☐ Myself ☐ Student: _____

	Excellent		Average		Needs Work
Speaking Style					
Good posture 5	4	3	2	I
Smiles 5	4	3	2	I
Eye contact 5	4	3	2	I
Clear voice, good volume...............................5	4	3	2	I
Shows excitement (uses some gestures and voice variety).......5	4	3	2	I
Report Content					
Overall content...5	4	3	2	I
Clear organization 5	4	3	2	I
Interesting introduction 5	4	3	2	I
Lots of details and examples 5	4	3	2	I
Gives a conclusion...5	4	3	2	I
Tells about references 5	4	3	2	I

What did you like best about the report? _____

_____

_____

Overall rating: I'd give this person a 5   4   3   2   I

TIME MANAGEMENT WORKSHEET

TASK	POINTS	DUE DATE
Choose topic	8 points for topic 1 point for each alternate topic (maximum 2 points)	_____ _____
Develop questions	1 point for each question (maximum 5 points)	_____
Identify possible references	**Total points possible: 15**	
Collect information	4 points per reference (maximum 20 points)	_____
Turn in note cards or reference pages	**Total points possible: 20**	
Write outline	10 points for format (main topics, indented subtopics)	_____
● Group and organize ideas	5 points for neatness	_____
● Add introduction and conclusion	5 points for grouping, logic, and completeness **Total points possible: 20**	_____
Write and revise first draft	5 points for completing first draft	_____
● Include bibliography	5 points for revising first draft 5 points for bibliography **Total points possible: 15**	_____ _____
Complete final draft		
● Include cover	5 points for cover with all parts	_____
● Include bibliography	5 points for neatness (clean, legible, margins)	_____
● Type, word process, or write in ink	5 points for format (headings, indents, etc.)	_____
	15 points for completing final draft -1 point for each spelling or grammar error	_____
	Total points possible: 30	

TOPIC, QUESTIONS, AND REFERENCES APPROVAL FORM

Complete this approval sheet and submit it to your teacher.

Name_____ Class_____ Period_____ Date_____

TOPIC

My first choice topic is: _____

My second choice topic is: _____

My third choice topic is: _____

☐ Topic Approved by Teacher   Date: _____

  1. Question: _____

  Possible reference: _____

  2. Question: _____

  Possible reference: _____

  3. Question: _____

  Possible reference: _____

  4. Question: _____

  Possible reference: _____

  5. Question: _____

  Possible reference: _____

☐ Questions Approved by Teacher   Date: _____

☐ References Approved by Teacher Date: _____

Teacher's Comments:_____

_____

_____

_____

_____

SPECIAL REFERENCE PAGE

Name_____ Reference Page No.:_____

BIBLIOGRAPHICAL INFORMATION: PRINT
....

(book, magazine, brochure, newspaper, etc.)

Title: _____

Author (last name first): _____

Publisher (for book; write city, company, year):_____

Article title (magazine or newspaper): _____

Date of publication (magazine or newspaper): _____

Pages: _____

BIBLIOGRAPHICAL INFORMATION: PERSON
....

(personal or telephone interview)

Name: _____ Title: _____

Telephone:_____ Date of interview: _____

BIBLIOGRAPHICAL INFORMATION: OTHER
....

(film, video, database, CD-ROM, multi-media, etc.)

Description:_____

Title: _____

Notes that help to answer my question(s): _____

_____

_____

_____

_____

_____

_____

Other interesting notes: _____

_____

_____

_____

Continued on another page? Yes ☐ No ☐

REPORT OUTLINE

I. Introduction

    A. _____

    B. _____

    C. _____

    D. _____

II. First main topic: _____

    A. _____

    B. _____

    C. _____

    D. _____

III. Second main topic: _____

    A. _____

    B. _____

    C. _____

    D. _____

IV. Third main topic: _____

    A. _____

    B. _____

    C. _____

    D. _____

V. Fourth main topic: _____

    A. _____

    B. _____

    C. _____

    D. _____

VI. Fifth main topic: _____

    A. _____

    B. _____

    C. _____

    D. _____

VII. Conclusion

    A. _____

    B. _____

    C. _____

    D. _____

Additional Readings and References

Crowell, Sheila C., and Ellen D. Kolba. *The Essay*. Educational Design Inc. New York, NY, 1985.

Crowell, Sheila C., and Ellen D. Kolba. *Practicing the Writing Process*. Educational Design Inc. New York, NY, 1985.

Dahlstrom, Lorraine M. *Writing Down the Days: 365 Creative Journaling Ideas for Young People*. Free Spirit Publishing Inc. Minneapolis, MN, 1990. A year's worth of journaling ideas, tied to the calendar year.

Monti, David, Michael T. Ganci, and Joseph A. Ganci. *Think and Write Books A through C*. Educational Design Inc. New York, NY, 1989.

Stock, Gregory. *The Book of Questions*. Workman Publishing Inc. New York, NY, 1987. The grown-up version of *The Kid's Book of Questions*. Many of the questions may be suitable for student journal topics.

Stock, Gregory. *The Kid's Book of Questions*. Workman Publishing Inc. New York, NY, 1988. An outstanding book for journal topics.

Other Books by the Author

Expanding Work Opportunities is a three mini-book series written for grades 6 to 10. It helps young students explore and identify their talents in three types of opportunities: neighborhood employment, self-employment, and volunteer or service work. Each area is discussed in a separate booklet. Write to Educational Design, 47 W. 13th, New York, NY 10011.

Looking for Leisure in All the Right Places offers new insight into the connection between work and leisure. This integrated theme is pursued by re-applying the principles used in self-directed job search programs to the search for leisure opportunities. An extensive assessment section helps students analyze their leisure interests, styles, and preferences. This leisure assessment process can help supply the writer with many new topics of interest. The program also emphasizes research skills including networking, researching by phone, surveying opinions, organizing search skills, and creatively identifying local resources and opportunities. These could all be used in a final leisure search report. Write to the author for details c/o Free Spirit Publishing Inc., 400 First Avenue North, Suite 616, Minneapolis, MN 55401.

Portfolio Workbook is a how-to book for students on the selection of samples, their organization, and their presentation in portfolio format and also orally. Available fall of 1994 from Free Spirit Publishing Inc., 400 First Avenue North, Suite 616, Minneapolis, MN 55401.

Teaching Is Dramatic presents theater games, improvisations, and skit work in a ready-to-use format. These activities can be used with any age group and in any subject. You might use them to prepare students for classroom drama activities, writing assignments, video productions, public speaking, and group work. The materials are designed for the non-drama educator or trainer. Formerly published by Ednicks Communications. Write to the author for details c/o Free Spirit Publishing Inc., 400 First Avenue North, Suite 616, Minneapolis, MN 55401.

Work Journal gives students a chance to examine the success of their job site through the process of journal writing. The journal encourages new workers to sharpen their critical observation and reflective thinking habits. Students involved in work experience are asked to analyze the success factors in their work settings. Write to EBSCO Curriculum Materials, Box 1943, Birmingham, AL 35201.

Write into a Job uses "writing as a process" to link vocational and academic skills during résumé writing. Résumé alternatives are also illustrated for students with limited writing ability. Advanced techniques related to desktop publishing design are included. Effective use of the résumé in a job search is illustrated throughout. For more information, write to the author c/o Free Spirit Publishing Inc., 400 First Avenue North, Suite 616, Minneapolis, MN 55401.

(w)Rites of Passage is a work in progress. It is designed for adults who wish to record and explore their life's meaning through journal writing. For more information, write to the author c/o Free Spirit Publishing Inc., 400 First Avenue North, Suite 616, Minneapolis, MN 55401.

Index

T

Television advertisements. *See* Advertising writing; Script writing

Term papers. *See* Research papers

Thank-you letters, 10

Theater games, 31-34

book about, 94

and nonverbal communication, 26

See also Drama; Script writing

Time limits, as power writing, 9

Time management

and research papers, 47, 58, 87

worksheet, 87

Tongue twisters, as warm-up for public speaking, 29

V

Variety, and language enrichment, 2, 5. *See also* Flexibility

Visualizing, and speech writing, 4

W

Word-association, power writing as, 9

Word counting

and journal writing, 13-17, 65

and power writing, 9-10

Work opportunities. *See* Jobs

Writer's block, 9

Writing

four-step process 4, 11-12, 26, 28, 62-64, 73-74

original vs. copy work, 54

See also Drafting; Editing; Prewriting; Revising

About the Author

artin Kimeldorf is the author of over 15 books and reports on the topics of job finding, leisure finding, community service, journal writing, and recreational drama. He holds Bachelor of Science degrees in technology education and liberal arts from Oregon State University, and a Master's Degree in special education from Portland State University. He received the Literati Award from the *International Journal of Career Management* for Best Paper of the Year and has won other awards for teaching and playwriting. His hobbies include wood carving, painting, and magic. Martin lives with his wife, Judy, and their dog, Mitzi, in Tumwater, Washington. He is interested in any comments or suggestions you might have about his works or inquiries about workshops and consultations. Write to him c/o Free Spirit Publishing Inc., 400 First Avenue North, Suite 616, Minneapolis, MN 55401.

The Free Spirited Classroom™ Series

Books to make your classroom come alive . . .
and to make your job as a teacher easier and more fun

If you enjoy **Exciting Writing**, be sure to check out the other titles in this series:

TNT Teaching:
Over 200 Dynamite
Ways to Make Your Classroom Come Alive
written and illustrated by Randy Moberg

Hundreds of fresh, exciting ways to present the curriculum, plus new uses for media equipment—even a course in cartooning. Includes dozens of reproducible handout and transparency masters. Grades K–8.

160 pp., illust., s/c, 8 1/2" x 11"
ISBN 0-915793-64-4, $19.95

Doing the Days
A Year's Worth of Creative Journaling,
Drawing, Listening, Reading, Thinking, Arts
& Crafts Activities for Children Ages 8–12
By Lorraine M. Dahlstrom

A full year of journaling activities for beginning writers, plus over 1,000 more things to read, hear, talk about, think about, look at, draw, find, try, and fly. A total of 1,464 learning activities linked to the calendar year span all areas of the curriculum and stress whole language, cooperative learning, and critical thinking skills. Grades 3–6.

240 pp., illust., s/c, 8 1/2" x 11"
ISBN 0-915793-62-8, $21.95

To place an order or to request a free catalog, write or call:

Free Spirit Publishing Inc.
400 First Avenue North, Suite 616
Minneapolis, MN 55401-1730
1-800-735-7323
612-338-2068

THE BRIDGE OVER THE MAIN

How a Small Polish Boy Survived World War II in Germany

Written by

STAN DOMORADZKI

edited by

Salvatore Caputo

Published by
Olympia Press
Akeley, Minnesota

Produced by
Five Star Publications, Incorporated
Chandler, Arizona

the bridge over the main

Published 1999 by Olympia Press
Akeley, Minnesota
Produced by Five Star Publications, Incorporated
Chandler, Arizona
Printed in the United States of America

Requests for permissions should be addressed to:
Olympia Press
Akeley, MN.
P.O. Box 193, Akeley, MN. 56433

Library of Congress Cataloging-in-Publication Data
Domoradzki, Stan, 1927-
The Bridge Over The Main: how a small Polish boy survived World War II in Germany/Stan Domoradzki; edited by Salvatore Caputo.

p. cm.

ISBN 0-9667171-0-4

1. Domoradzki, Stan, 1927-. 2. World War, 1939-1945 – Prisoners and prisons, German. 3. World War, 1939-Personal narratives, Polish. 5. Boys – Poland – Biography. 6. Bavaria (Germany) – History, Military. I. Caputo, Salvatore. II. Title.
D805.G3D646 1999
940.54'7243'09433-dc21   98-37701
                                      CIP

Publishing consultant: Linda F. Radke
Editor: Salvatore Caputo
Cover design: Pamela I. Zirtzlaff-Teslow
Proofreader: Gail Baker, Sue DeFabis
Typesetting: T.G. Haynes